The Elements of
Nonsexist Usage

A Guide to Inclusive Spoken and Written English

Val Dumond

PRENTICE
HALL
PRESS

New York London Toronto Sydney Tokyo Singapore

First edition

Copyright © 1990 by Val Dumond

Prentice Hall Press

Simon & Schuster, Inc.
15 Columbus Circle
New York, NY 10023

Published by Prentice Hall Press

Manufactured in the United States of America

Prentice Hall and colophons are registered trademarks of
Simon & Schuster, Inc.

1   2   3   4   5   6   7   8   9   10

Library of Congress Cataloging-in-Publication Data

Dumond, Val.
    The elements of non-sexist usage: a guide to
inclusive spoken and written English/Val Dumond.
        p.   cm.
    Includes Index.
    ISBN 0-13-368911-5 : $4.95
    1. English language—Usage. 2. Nonsexist language. I.
Title.
PE1460.D78   1991
428—dc20   90-26948
                                                CIP

Contents

Contents

Introduction

This is a guide to writing and using words to eliminate sexist language. Such an objective not only is possible to accomplish, it also is very simple to accomplish.

Over the past 20 years, several contrived words have been offered to solve the problem of sexism in language. Most of these offerings are what they appear to be—contrived to cover a gap in the English language. They include *she/he, (s)he, co, cos, sher, shim, herm, heris, tey, tem, ter(s), ve, ver,* . . . and the list goes on. However, it isn't necessary to go to these lengths in order to eliminate or at least reduce sexism in today's language. And the need to make an attempt is increasing.

Modern business people recognize the fact that half of today's consumers are women. Some leaders of historically male-oriented companies are discovering more and more women in their ranks, both as employees and as clients. The need to deal equally with men and women brings into focus the need to adopt language usage that includes both sexes.

Strong evidence is surfacing to support the suspicion that language directly affects behavior. Language that disparages women is demeaning to half the population and therefore is connected to the growing rate of violence against women. A direct link exists between verbal abuse and physical abuse. What starts with words can and often does escalate to acting out.

Government agencies (municipal, state, and federal), in an effort to satisfy affirmative-action and equal-opportunity programs, require those doing business with them to adhere to terminology that includes both men and women. This terminology is used to label the kind of language that refuses to discriminate according to gender. It is variably called *nonsexist, genderless, gender-free, gender-neutral, inclusive, nonbiased,* or *unbiased language.* Slight shadings of difference are indicated by the terminology. *Nonsexist, genderless, gender-free,* and *gender-neutral* mean that inappropriate references to gender are omitted. *Inclusive* means that language does not exclude, either by direct reference or implication, one gender or the other. *Nonbiased* or *unbiased* simply shows the words are not intended to reflect gender bias. All the terms mean basically the same thing: words need to be chosen carefully to eliminate inappropriate gender implications.

This book is arranged simply, to provide guidelines to nonsexist language. Included in the Appendix is an alphabetic guide to alternative terms for sexist words. Throughout the book are examples of the many simple ways to correct sexist language.

Chapters are arranged for quick reference to solve problems as the needs arise. Use this book as a writing tool, a reference to ensure that your written ideas are free of sexist implication. Use it as a general language tool by reading it through. You'll find the overview a help in acquiring simple techniques to reduce sexism in writing and speaking.

Mother always taught, "Good communicators don't need to use profanity to make their meanings clear." Her progeny now contend, "Neither do good communicators need to supply gender when none is indicated, or when to do so excludes half the population."

Keep this guidebook close when you prepare ads, news copy, sales literature, training material, customer letters, or orders. If you come up with a problem the book doesn't answer, please send it to me in care of the publisher to receive a personal reply.

1 Think Before You Write

Writing so that you won't exclude or provoke half your readers need not be difficult. Here are just a few ideas to keep in mind when putting words together.

Words are symbols. Words represent things. Some of the things are objects; others are concepts. A word like *cup* represents an item that generally is recognized as a receptacle for fluids. It can have many shapes, forms, and colors, but it always serves this same function. A word like *freedom*, on the other hand, represents an idea, a concept. Its interpretation relies completely on the experience and beliefs of the interpreter.

Now we come to the word *man*. Its denotative meaning is "an adult male human." When the word is used, that is the mental picture that is formed. The picture is what simultaneously represents a conceptual meaning to the interpreter. Since a female picture does not come to mind when the word *man* is used, it would follow that *man* does not represent in any way a female human. Yes, past usage has been accepted, representing *man* as inclusive of all humans. Still, *man* does not mean "woman." Therefore, the word should be used only when an adult male human is meant. Ways to correct and write around this problem are offered in Chapter 3.

When the gender of an object is nonexistent or unknown, there is no reason to attach a supposed gender. If you are talking about a doctor whose identity is not given, do not assume the doctor is a *he*.

Find other words to symbolize exactly what you mean. Solutions to the problem of the assumed pronoun are discussed further in Chapter 4. Substituting the word *person* every time such a problem arises is not the answer!

Equally important as the pronoun usage are the many words in our language that *imply* gender, either through endings or through general cultural usage. What mind-picture appears when encountering the words *teacher, professor, nurse, doctor, secretary,* or *boss?* Many words loudly imply gender when they should not. The words themselves are fine; we should stop associating them with gender-specific images.

Sexism is often introduced into language through the use of a suffix. Adding *ess* or *ette* onto an otherwise neutral noun indicates a feminine adjustment to a masculine word and should be avoided in nonsexist language. There is no need to use *heiress* or *shepherdess* when *heir* and *shepherd* are perfectly complete words. Endings and implications are the subject matter of Chapter 5.

Some words that diminish and demean are used in sexist language, as in the use of *girl* when an adult woman is meant or of *tomato* or *chick* to refer to a woman. In some instances the word *lady* is used to demean. *Lady* should be used as an adjective only if it would be equally fitting to use *gentleman* in a similar male instance. Discussion of this problem appears in Chapter 6.

Business people could be losing many dollars each time they use sexist terms, such as *lady of the house* or *Dear Housewife.* They also could be incorrectly addressing employees as *salesmen, businessmen,* or *admen.* Or they may be erroneously referring to *the secretary . . . she* or *the supervisor . . . he.* And what do we do about *Dear Sir* and *Gentlemen* to introduce our letters? New trends in business writing, in-house and out, are addressed in Chapter 7.

Many cultural habits contribute to sexism in our language. For instance, the indiscriminate tendency to add *man* to many words is one unfortunate idiosyncrasy of English, as in words like *salesman, chairman, journeyman, spokesman,* and *fireman.* Then there are words with separate cultural meanings, such as *patron, bachelor,* and *master* (as in academic degrees). *Patron* will never be equated with *matron;* the words have distinctly different meanings. Oddly enough, a female patron of the arts sometimes is referred to as a *patroness!* Think about it. What to do with such deeply ingrained sexist word usage is approached in Chapter 8.

Throughout this guidebook are some very simple ways to write around sexist language. These include substituting ungendered words, using plurals, changing to first or second person (or third person plural), repeating the noun, omitting the pronoun altogether, and substituting *the,* as well as rewriting the sentence to avoid the problem. Examples of improper, sexist usage are shown in the text preceded by the letter *S* (meaning Sexist). These are followed by examples of preferred, nonsexist usage, shown preceded by the letter *N* (meaning Nonsexist). In the back of the book, listed alphabetically, is a list of sexist job titles and other terms, along with nonsexist alternatives, for quick and easy reference.

Achieving nonsexist language in daily communication may take some effort at first. But like most newly learned skills, it becomes easier as new habits begin to form. Soon you will be able to spot sexism in the communication of others as easily as you avoid it in your own.

Read on—and as you become aware of language and how it reflects more than the surface definition, you will realize how important word meanings are to all those who read and hear your words.

2 Image! Word! Action!

Have you ever heard the lament, "I know what I want to say, I just don't know how to say it"? We all sometimes experience this loss for words: we're seeing an image that we can't attach words to. While we may not be sure which comes first, the chicken or the egg, we do know about images and words. Images preceded words, in civilization and in our daily communications.

When words are spoken, at least three sets of meanings can be attached to them. First, there is the meaning that the speaker attaches to the image being defined; second, there is that given by the listener according to experience and understanding; and third, there is the dictionary meaning. (Occasionally, however, a word is used that is not found in the dictionary but still carries a sensory meaning.)

The world of communication calls that third meaning *denotative*. The denotative meaning is the general understanding about the word among people in the language business. The "dictionary says" kinds of definitions (which sometimes reflect the experience of the dictionary writer/editor) give us a standardized meaning for most words.

We are told that of the 600,000 or so words in the English language, the average, educated adult uses about 2,000. Of these, there are about 500 words that carry more than 14,000 meanings, which means that most of these words have at least three or more meanings, and some words are given as many as 100

5

meanings! It is no wonder we "average, educated" adults find difficulty in transferring definitions of meanings to each other.

How does this affect the sexism in our language?

Most of the English language was developed and defined by men. Male scholars recorded grammar rules, syntax design, and word definitions. Early male scholars developed the early recorded language and then taught language skills, primarily to men. Little wonder that the language reflects a male point of view.

Words are the tools of communication. Words can convey ideas of how people are *expected* to act, how they carry out what are considered stereotyped roles. Words can be used as weapons—as ways to hurt people, ways to inflict emotional harm through verbal abuse. Words can affect the emotional reaction of the listener in a subliminal, subconscious way, doing their damage over a period of time by reinforcing negative self-image.

STEREOTYPING

People behave according to their self-perception. Sometimes the perception develops over time according to the way other people perceive them and communicate this perception. When people perceive themselves as clowns, they tend to act like clowns. When males perceive themselves as tough, powerful men, they carry themselves proudly, strongly, and powerfully. When women perceive themselves as weak, passive, and submissive, they behave in powerless ways.

Americans love to attach labels to things, to pigeonhole and name them. Often the first question asked of a pregnant woman is, "Do you want a boy or girl?" The first question upon a new birth is, "Which is it, boy or girl?" The second question usually is, "What are you going to name her (or him)?" When adults talk to children, they like to ask, "How old are you? What grade are you in? Where do you go to school?" When adults are introduced to other adults, they ask such things as, "Where are you from? What do you do for a living?" We need to know where to pigeonhole people from the very first. We seldom ask philosophical questions such as, "How do you feel about music? What are your favorite books?"

Sexist stereotyping occurs when we slant our questions according to our own perceptions. Here's how sexist role stereotyping works: In your mind, picture a doctor, school superintendent, bank president, nurse, teacher, and secretary. Weren't the first three men and the second three women? That is sexist stereotyping. We tend to think of certain roles *belonging* to certain kinds of people, a certain gender, a certain economic pigeonhole, and certain behavioral characteristics.

The result of stereotypical thinking is circular bias. As the hearer of the words, the pictures we draw in our minds come automatically, instantaneously, and reflect our beliefs about these stereotypes. As the speaker, our words reflect our own stereotyping.

The meaning of *stereotype* is "an unvarying form or pattern; a fixed or conventional notion or conception, as of a person, group, idea, etc., held by a number of people, and allowing for no individuality, critical judgment . . . not original or individualized." The original word referred to a metal printing plate used to mold type—that is, something that is thought out and created once, then used to reproduce the same concept over and over, without thinking.

When stereotyping results in role pigeonholing, we enter a world of sexist labeling that affects the way we behave. If we label our business leaders as *business-*

men, we are setting up a criterion for business people to behave as men do, implying that if you are a woman, you need to behave as men do in order to become a businessman.

The tendency is to stereotype men in aggressive, active, powerful ways and women in submissive, passive, nurturing ways. We draw these definitions from biology classes, where we are taught that men and women *tend* to behave in these ways. What we fail to realize is that all of us are capable of all these behaviors whether we are men or women. We just carry the tendencies around in a variety of proportions. Some men have very little of the feminine traits of nurturing, passive, submissive behavior; some women have very little of the masculine traits of aggressive, active, powerful behavior. Men tend to display more of the masculine traits, women more of the feminine traits. However, there are exceptions: we all know men who act submissively and women who act aggressively.

By stereotyping roles of activity in the workplace, we further restrict the scope of us all to expand our vocational horizons. Some women excel in trade skills (what we traditionally call "nontraditional" jobs for women), and many men excel in nurturing skills (what we traditionally call "women's work").

By eliminating the telltale endings on certain jobs, we can reduce the tendency to *think* about jobs as having gender preference. We don't need to add *ess* or *ette* to certain standard (male) words to indicate a woman's role, as with *waitress, actress, poetess, authoress, bachelorette,* or *majorette.*

There's nothing wrong with calling the person who waits on tables a *waiter* or a person who performs in plays an *actor,* whether male or female. The bias against the *ess* and *ette* endings stems from the hit-and-miss way in which they are applied. Many job titles are untouched by the gender implications, including *journalist, writer, plumber, trucker,* and *executive.*

VERBAL ABUSE

Words can be used as weapons or as healers, depending on the choice of verbiage and the manner in which they are spoken. Even such unobtrusive words as *mother* and *baby* can hurt others if used with a demeaning tone of voice.

Verbal jabs of "cry baby," "mother's boy," and "your mother!" often are used with the intent to hurt. Children particularly are good at this. Watch a playground for a few minutes and you'll see them using words to hurt others (probably because they know that physical attacks would threaten their own well-being).

Words—sexist and otherwise—can be used without the threat of bodily harm. Sometimes, taken to greater intensity, they induce bodily harm. Most sexist words, however, are hurled between grown men and women and, as often as not, come from women's mouths. Men and women label the verbally abusive woman as a *witch* or as *bitchy, catty, venomous,* or *spiteful.* The verbally abusive man is *in charge, controlling, demanding, belligerent, combative, domineering,* or *hard-hitting.*

Back in childhood, we started this verbal abuse by sneering when we talked about little boys acting as *girls* or little girls acting as *tomboys.* Somehow, the words came out to mean something worse for the *sissified* little boys than it did for the *boyish* little girls.

Researchers are discovering definite links between verbal and physical abuse. They are finding that some men who verbally abuse women are just biding time until they escalate to physical abuse (if no intervention or help occurs along the way). Why not? When men talk down to women, demeaning them with words, the images in their heads are of women who are valueless, who *ask for* the putdowns. When men regard women as objects, things, and possessions, they will behave in a way towards women that reflects their beliefs; hence the *battered woman.* Likewise, when women regard men as the source of all their troubles, the weak little boys that require strong mothering, they will behave in ways that reflect *their* beliefs; hence, the *hen-pecked husband.*

If there were a cure for this malaise of our society, we would be showering the discoverer of it with riches. However, people being people, men will continue to abuse women verbally (most likely to shore up their own sense of importance) and women will continue to treat men in kind (to give themselves a forced sense of superiority).

The importance of this knowledge is that when we feel secure about ourselves, we don't have to take out feelings of inferiority on others. We don't have to make ourselves feel more important, or more powerful, by knocking others down. We don't have to get our power highs by making others feel weak and meaningless.

No verbal abuse leads to physical abuse overnight. An insidious, long-term process of devaluation takes place over a period of time. When we can recognize the simple abuse of such terms as *my girl, girlie, just-like-a-woman,* and *mama's boy,* we can acknowledge the demeaning implications behind them and erase them from common usage.

One-time usage does little by itself, but repetition over years takes its toll. How often do we hear a battered woman confess that her batterer had been talking to her in demeaning terms and treating her like a possession for years before the physical battering took place?

It all begins with words. While we acknowledge the healing power of words, the value of words to motivate and strengthen, the ability of words to soothe and calm, we are slow to acknowledge the killing power of words when used maliciously.

PATRONIZING WORDS

When are words patronizing? Some words are of themselves patronizing. Others, in condescending usage or emphasis, become so. Talking down to children is easily identified as condescending or patronizing. Other patronizing acts include talking very slowly in one-syllable words to an older person or treating hearing- or sight-impaired people as unintelligent.

Sexist patronization is almost an oxymoron, in that the root word comes from *patron* ("defender, protector"), which in turn derives from the Latin *pater*, or "father." The dictionary definition of *patronize* is "to be kind or helpful to, but in a haughty or snobbish way, as if dealing with an inferior."

When a father talks down to a little girl, he usually is playing the domination routine, assuming the role of the powerful benefactor. The same holds true when the father figure is the male boss talking down to a woman clerk or secretary, a male minister talking down to a woman parishioner, or a male principal talking patronizingly to a woman teacher. Whether or not the husband is talking to the wife or the brother talking to the sister, if there is a tone of condescension (talking down) there is patronization. And, yes, women can patronize too.

Most patronizing remarks go unchallenged. They draw their abusive strength from subversion, for the very fact that they are not pointed out and acknowledged as patronizing.

Simone de Beauvoir, the French author who wrote *The Second Sex,* clarified the roots of male dominance in our culture and our language by directing our attention to the men who founded and developed Western religion, wrote the Bible, took charge of exploring the world, and managed the world's commerce, established its governments, fought its wars, and reserved the leadership of education and the arts for themselves. She contends that to read history is to read the history of men. Little wonder history is referred to as the development of *mankind.* It literally disregards, sometimes by intent but surely by design, the overwhelming contributions of women along the way from caves to penthouses. It disregards women's contributions to music, art, literature, government, education, commerce, and religion, placing any small mentions of women in single paragraphs, sometimes in a single sentence.

To include women in a word like *man* or *mankind* suggests that they don't merit their own word, that they must be content to be included in the generic *man.* Women become conditioned to borrowing men's descriptions, men's definitions, men's titles, men's work, and even men's ideas. The result of this emphasis on men's contributions to civilization is the repetitious message that women are also-rans, second-class citizens, tag-alongs, things. When this verbal abuse is carried on for years by a husband, father, or son, a woman may grow to consider herself worthless. It then may be a small step from verbal abuse to physical abuse, since the woman may believe she deserves whatever she gets.

And it all begins with words, carried down in history and through history. The implication of women's inferiority is now being met with resistance from most women, who are demanding their place alongside men in history, in life.

HERSTORY (HISTORY REWRITTEN)

To provide the flavor of what it means to be a woman and be aware of the words that place women in the runner-up slot of the human race, the following rewriting of history is offered. Whether you are a woman or a man, notice your feelings as you read it. You may be surprised by how these words make you feel.

An Awareness Experience

We are going to reverse the generic term man. *Think, instead, of the generic term* woman. *Think of the future of womankind, which, of course, includes both women and men. Sense that meaning to you— as a woman, as a man.*

Think of it always being this way, every day of your life. Feel the omnipresence of woman *and feel the nonpresence of* man. *Absorb what this tells you about the importance and value of being woman, of being man.*

First look back to the beginnings of the civilization of woman. Remember your early ancestral relatives? Cro-magnon woman, Java woman, Neanderthal woman—all cavewomen (which includes men, of course). Recall that early woman invented fire and discovered the use of stone tools near the beginnings of the Stone Age. Remember that what separates woman from other species is that she can think.

Which gives us thinking woman, industrial woman, democratic woman, working woman, creative woman, and now even mechanical woman. There is the common woman and the woman-on-the-street.

Recall your history. Recall how feudal woman spread into Europe and built castles, how mythical woman developed around the Aegean and Mediterra-

nean Seas—those mythical women who had wild adventures with strange creatures while their husbands sat at home and waited.

Follow history through religious woman, starting with Eve and Sarah and continuing through to crusading woman. Know that the all-knowing, all-powerful God is female, as are the leaders of Her church.

And remember discovering woman and exploring woman—who had adventures sailing around the world and discovering new continents, new worlds. And recall their ships, named Nino, Pinto, and Santo Paulo (they always named their ships for men to remind them who was waiting at home).

Look now at colonial woman, those brave women who carved a civilization out of wilderness, met and befriended the Indians, then made witches out of the men who gave them trouble.

Let us look at pioneering woman—those courageous women who crossed the mountains, fought the bears, panned for gold, built railroads, discovered oil, and tamed the forests.

Regard the women of art, music, and literature—women who recorded life in oils and watercolors and gave the world sonatas, symphonies, novels, poetry—art in all its forms.

Now we come to industrial women, businesswomen who became the mothers of our country and who sent their daughters to war, twice. Those women who developed the fields of medicine and law.

Understand that your physician is probably a woman and feel comfortable when she tells you that a body is just a body after all. Know that your attorney is probably a woman and that you can entrust your financial and business affairs to her.

Recall that everything you have ever read, all your life, uses only feminine pronouns—she and her—meant to include both girls and boys, women and men. *Recall that most of the voices on the radio and most faces on TV are those of women, especially when important events are covered or important products are sold.*

Know that you have only two male senators representing you in Washington, and that only 27 of 435 representatives are male; no men sit in the President's cabinet; no man has ever served as President; and only one man has ever sat on the Supreme Court. Know that men, including the recent male candidate for the vice presidency, are oddities in the political world. Women are the natural leaders, the power centers, the prime movers.

Man, whose natural role is husband and father, fulfills himself through nurturing children and making the home a refuge for woman. This is only natural to balance the biological role of woman, who devotes her entire body to the race during pregnancy—the most revered power known to woman (including, of course, man).

Understand the obvious biological explanation for woman as the ideal. By design, the female reproductive center is compact and internal, protected by her body. The male is so exposed that he must be protected from outside attack to assure the perpetuation of the race.

Thus, by nature, males are more passive than females. If the male denies feeling passive and inferior, he is unconsciously rejecting his masculinity. Therapy is thus indicated to help him adjust to his own nature. Of course, therapy is administered by a woman who has the education and wisdom to facilitate openness, leading to the male's self-growth and actualization.

To help him feel into his defensive emotionalism, the male is invited to get in touch with the child in him. He can remember how his sister could run, climb, and ride horseback unencumbered. Obviously, since she is free to move, she is encouraged to develop her body and mind in preparation for her active responsibilities of adult womanhood. She is free to train and enter the exciting world of athletics, earning fantastic sums in professional sports as well as earning the adulation of a nation's youth.

Male vulnerability needs female protection, so man is taught the caring, less active virtues of homemaking. He is encouraged to keep his body lean and attractive and to dream of getting married, of belonging to a special woman—changing his name to hers, replacing that stilted "master" with the respectful "mister." He dreams of cooking for her and keeping his house clean for her.

"I now pronounce you woman and husband" are magical words he longs to hear. Then he waits for the time of fulfillment when "his woman" gives him a girl child to carry on her family name. He knows that if it is a boy child he has failed somehow—but he can try again.

And so life has been through the ages. Our foremothers paved the way for us today; we must thank them.

Are you getting the feelings of being a woman, of being a man? Are you aware of the words that bring the ideas to you in order to evoke the feelings? They're only words—or are they?

3 *Man* Does Not Mean *Woman*

Great attention is given in today's language to the meaning of the words *man* and *mankind*. Some contend that *man* has become used historically to mean the entire human population—both women and men. *Mankind* likewise has been used to represent all of humanity.

Take another look. *Homo sapiens* is the Latin scientific identification of a biological species that includes both sexes, male and female. The word *man* in the English language specifically identifies only one of them, the male. Another word, *woman,* is used to define the other, the female of the species. If you wish to delve into derivatives, you will find a question as to the origin of this word. Linguists generally conclude it is not a diminution of *man,* but rather derives from the Old English meaning of "wife of man."

Similarly, words denoting the sex of a human are *male* and *female.* The word *male* identifies the masculine sex of *Homo sapiens*; the word *female,* however, is believed to derive from the French word *femelle,* meaning "small woman." Because of the spelling resemblance to *male,* the meaning has been extended to "Homo sapiens of feminine gender."

Man does not mean "woman," nor should it be so used. In the interest of accuracy, men are masculine, women are feminine.

Many alternatives are available to replace the word *man* when referring to all human beings. Likewise, there are alternatives to using *mankind* to refer to both woman- and mankind collectively.

Examples:

S: Man has inhabited the earth for thousands of years.
N: Humans have inhabited the earth for thousands of years.

S: Wherever there is freedom, mankind will survive.
N: Wherever there is freedom, humankind will survive.

S: All men are created equal.
N: All people are created equal.

As demonstrated above, it is possible to emphasize precise meaning with a more accurate term. Now the reader or listener is absolutely certain the speaker isn't referring only to male people.

All human beings are not men. Therefore, to use such general terms as *industrial man, political man,* and *social man* is to fall into the generic man trap. The history of man is also the history of women.

Avoid using *man* to refer to the typical human: *working man, man of the world, man of goodwill, man on the street.* It is just as easy—and more accurate—to use *worker, worldly* or *cosmopolitan citizen, peacemaker,* or *average person.*

MALE/FEMALE

The terms *male* and *female* refer to the sex of an individual and should be used only when referring to sex distinctions. These words are used to denote the sex of *any* living thing, from trees to animals, including people.

Examples:

Females live longer than males. (This is a bit clinical, but is accepted in biological circles.)

Women live longer than men. (Better, as long as you are referring only to people.)

Females of the human species bear the children; males fertilize the seed.

But not:

The string quartet includes two females. (No, no, no!)

Better:

The string quartet includes two women. (Acceptable only if this is an exceptional case.)

Best:

The string quartet is made up of two women and two men.

WOMAN

A woman is a female human, generally considered to be over the age of puberty. Younger female humans are referred to as *girls*.

Woman, used as a modifier, should be used only if it is required to clarify meaning.

Example:

The cab driver picked up the fare at Center Street.

Not:
The woman cab driver picked up the fare at
  Center Street.

Unless there was an unusual circumstance:
The woman cab driver picked up the fare at
  Center Street and was hit over the head and
  threatened by the man passenger.

or:
The woman cab driver asked the fare she
  picked up at Center Street to drive her to the
  hospital, where the cabbie gave birth to
  twins.

In American society today, some characteristics are
acceptable only for women, such as gentleness, beauty, and softness. When applied to men, these characteristics have been rejected. On the other hand, many
characteristics associated by usage with men, when
applied to women, take on positive meaning; these
include dignity, strength, fortitude, courage, and
assertiveness. These role expectations, long held in
America, are changing and no longer are being
accepted without question.

Women are not asking to be called men. In fact,
women are asking *not* to be called men, not to be
included in the term *man.* Further, women are asking
that jobs and elected posts be described by terms that
include women, or at least do not exclude them: *council members, legislators, sales agents, journalists,* and
business executives, rather than *councilmen, Congressmen, salesmen, newsmen,* and *businessmen.*

DESCRIBING WOMEN

When describing women, avoid describing their
appearance in terms of their sexuality or femininity

unless the same or equivalent terms would be applied to men in the same situation.

> *Not acceptable:*
> Slender, radiant, blond (worse yet, *blonde*),
>   vivacious, stunning, beautiful, attractive, pert,
>   gorgeous, lovely.

When describing women, select detail carefully and honestly, asking, "Would the other sex be so described?" A man is seldom described according to what he is wearing or by the color of his hair.

When referring to women, avoid trivializing verbs, such as *ruffle, squeal, simper,* and *whimper.* Women are perceived traditionally and mistakenly as passive. The careful writer will not contribute to perpetuating this erroneous idea.

ANOTHER KIND OF MAN

Not all words incorporating the syllable *man* refer to the male human. Many English words derive from the Latin word *manus,* meaning *hand*—such as *manual, manuscript, manufacture, manage,* and *manipulate.* Interestingly, this Latin word has a linguistic masculine gender. Use of these derivative words technically escape the label of sexism, although the implication lingers via reference to hands as masculine.

GENERIC MAN

Be specific as often as you can; avoid generalizations. This has always been good advice to writers. When referring to *man* as a species, use *Homo sapiens, human society, ancestors, forebears, people, humans,* or *humankind.*

Other uses of *man* can be substituted by nonsexist terms.

> *Man* as verb: work, serve, operate, staff, run.
>
> *Man* as prefix (*mankind, manpower, man-hours, man-made*): humanity, human-powered, muscle-powered, workhours, artificial. A *manhole* accurately identified is a utility cover!
>
> *Man* as suffix (*spokesman*): spokesperson, representative, speaker.
>
> *Man* in the chair: convener, president, presider, leader, coordinator, director, or simply chair.
>
> *Men* as people (*Englishmen, Frenchmen*): the English, the French, Russians, Italians, laity, citizens, people.
>
> *Men* as public servants: representatives, members, legislators, senators, leaders, directors.
>
> *Men* at work: attendants, repairers, deliverers, agents, working people, workers, laborers.

4 All About Pronouns

A pronoun is a word that refers to and replaces a noun or other pronoun. First-person pronouns are genderless (*I, we, me, us, our, ours*), as are second-person pronouns (*you, your, yours*). Third-person pronouns are the ones that offer the sexist difficulties: *he, she, it, they, him, her, them, his, hers, its, their,* and *theirs*.

As long as we use the genders accurately, no problem exists. When we refer to a boy, we refer to *him*. Likewise, when we refer to a girl, we refer to *her*. It's when we refer to someone whom we don't know and thus can't accurately identify by gender that we get into trouble.

For a long time, usage has accepted masculine pronouns as common gender representatives for both masculine and feminine nouns. The masculine also has been used when the noun's gender is unknown or unclear. However, increasing numbers of *she*'s are objecting to being addressed as *he*'s.

> *If you say:*
> "Everyone is required to carry his identification," you have excluded the women who need their identification.
> *Instead, write or say:*
> "Everyone is required to carry identification."
>
> *Do not say:*
> A teacher inspires her receptive students.

23

A lawyer likes to win his cases.
A nurse is vigilant on her shift.
A police officer must keep his body fit.

It is much better to say:
A teacher inspires receptive students.
A lawyer likes to win cases.
A nurse is vigilant during working hours.
A police officer must keep a fit body.

NOTE TO GRAMMATICAL PURISTS

A note to the grammatical purist who has trouble accepting the idea that *he* does not include the feminine. The evolution of language in America includes much usage that is traced back to middle European roots. In those centuries of evolution, most early language usage applied only to the visible male. Men were feudal lords; men conducted business; men led religious orders; men were privy to education; men, in short, pretty much ran things.

Women were somewhere down the social ladder, mixed in with serfs and real estate. They were chattels, possessions, and therefore without status as individuals, persons, entities with rights. Contracts and other early writings excluded women automatically; women were of no legal concern. Early writings therefore used only the *he* to refer to human beings in the third person, human beings who were indeed men.

The idea that "we've always done it that way" doesn't carry enough weight to keep using an obviously masculine word to refer to all people, as if feminine people didn't matter. The implied meaning shouts too loudly to too many women in today's culture.

Several ways suggest themselves to avoid sexism of pronouns. No single technique will work in all situations; the following is simply a menu from which to choose a way to avoid the awkward *he/she*, the over-worked *person,* or sexist terminology.

1. Group words to use a plural pronoun properly.

2. Delete or omit the pronoun.

3. Use the word *the* in place of the pronoun.

4. Repeat the noun.

5. Use the passive verb form.

6. Change the sentence to use the first- or second-person pronoun.

7. Use the word *one* instead of the exclusive *he.*

8. Recast the sentence to change the subject.

9. Use singular nouns that take plural pronouns.

10. Only as a last-ditch effort, use both masculine and feminine pronouns (*he or she, his or hers*).

GROUP WORDS TO USE A PLURAL PRONOUN PROPERLY

When it is necessary to use a pronoun after an antecedent of undetermined or inclusive gender, try using plurals.

Examples:

S: A child should learn to tie his own shoes.
N: Children should learn to tie their own shoes.

S: The typical American knows his history.
N: Typical Americans know their history.

S: A Southerner likes his mint julep.
N: Southerners like their mint juleps.

Avoid giving gender to groups, thus implying a gender when it is inappropriate.

S: Every nurse should have her salary raised.
N: Nurses should have their salaries raised.

S: A doctor should have his own car.
N: Doctors should have their own cars.

She or *he* should be used only when reflected by reality. If the lawyer is a woman: *the lawyer called her secretary.* If the clerk is a man: *the clerk checked his inventory.*

Remember: nongender terms should not be used with masculine pronouns unless only males are indicated. These include such words as *baby, student, American, politician, Southerner, Italian, voter, slave, farmer, child,* and *parent.*

Example:

S: An American should salute his flag.
N: An American should salute the flag.
Americans should salute their flag.

Likewise, keep in mind:
A sage is a wise person (not necessarily male).
Man didn't discover fire—people did.
All pioneers were not men; half of our
ancestors were women!
Half of the American population are women!

DELETE OR OMIT THE PRONOUN

In many cases pronouns are used superfluously. Many sentences may read just as well, if not better, without a pronoun. We tend to overuse these little words just because they're available.

Examples:

S: A voter should always use his common sense.
N: A voter should always use common sense.

S: A politician likes to offer his opinions.
N: A politician likes to offer opinions.

S: An expert barber is likely to indulge his customers.
N: An expert barber is likely to indulge customers.

There are other ways to eliminate sexist pronouns. One is to reword the sentence by changing the subject.

Examples:

S: A lawyer who wants to win his case will do his homework.
N: Homework is important to the lawyer who wants to win a case.

S: Inventory can be taken alone by a clerk who has his own calculator.
N: A clerk who owns a calculator can take inventory alone.

USE THE WORD *THE* IN PLACE OF THE PRONOUN

Similar to omitting the offending pronoun is substituting *the*. Often the sentence will read better when the gender pronoun is thus replaced.

Examples:

S: A bookkeeper can get used to his detailed work.

N: A bookkeeper can get used to the detailed work.

S: A minister never tires of his nurturing duties.

N: A minister never tires of the nurturing duties.

REPEAT THE NOUN

Another way to eliminate the gender pronoun is to repeat the noun. This technique works particularly well in long sentences or when the noun and pronoun are widely separated by modifying phrases or clauses. Careful writers will discover this also clarifies understanding of who is doing what to whom.

Examples:

S: When the doctor arrived and saw the patient, he was worried. (Who was worried?)

N: When the doctor arrived and saw the patient, the doctor was worried.

S: The clerk who waited on the irate customer failed to see the humor in his problem. (Who had the problem? Clerk or customer?)

N: The clerk who waited on the irate customer failed to see the humor in the customer's problem.

It is better to repeat and be clear and accurate than to risk misunderstanding with a pronoun of obscure and misleading gender.

USE THE PASSIVE VOICE

This technique is probably the simplest way out of the sexist pronoun dilemma. When faced with a subject that could bring up a gender pronoun, rewrite the sentence to utilize the passive voice. Make the object the subject.

Examples:

S: The gardener uses his tools in his work.
N: The gardener's work is accomplished with the use of tools.

S: A good dancer chooses his choreographer carefully.
N: A choreographer must be chosen carefully by a good dancer.

S: Every secretary should know how to repair his typewriter.
N: Typewriter repair should be part of every secretary's training.

CHANGE THE SENTENCE TO USE THE FIRST- OR SECOND-PERSON PRONOUN

The use of first- or second-person pronouns is useful in many instances, especially when giving directions.

However, the choice of this technique must be made at the beginning of the writing process. Changing person in the middle of a piece does not result in good writing.

Decide at the beginning whether you can stick with the third-person pronoun or whether you need to consider transferring everything into either first or second person.

Examples:

S: The carpenter must care for her saw with regular cleaning.

N: As a carpenter, I must care for my saw with regular cleaning.

N: As a carpenter, you must care for your saw with regular cleaning.

S: A nurse treats all his patients with equal attention.

N: We treat all our patients with equal attention.

N: Treat all your patients with equal attention.

USE THE WORD *ONE* INSTEAD OF THE EXCLUSIVE *HE*

Practically self-explanatory, this is a consideration similar to substituting *the* or eliminating the pronoun. However, it remains another alternative, and occasions will arise when this technique is preferred to the others. Try using all three options before choosing the one that best fits the sentence meaning.

Examples:

S: A dancer's timing is critical; his moves must be well-timed.
N: A dancer's timing is critical; moves must be well-timed.
N: A dancer's timing is critical; one's moves must be well-timed.

S: The price of grapefruit determines her choice of breakfast menu.
N: The price of grapefruit determines the choice of breakfast menu.
N: The price of grapefruit determines one's choice of breakfast menu.

Conversely, the use of *one* as an indefinite noun can bring on other sexist pronoun problems. This can be eliminated by making the pronoun plural or by changing the subject.

Example:

S: A singer must establish his own voice range.
N: Singers must establish their own voice ranges.
N: A singer's voice range must be established by oneself.

RECAST THE SENTENCE TO CHANGE THE SUBJECT

Many situations arise where "you just can't get there from here." In other words, you may need to start over. When you cannot eliminate the sexist pronouns with a simple substitution or elimination, you may need to recast the sentence, the paragraph, or the whole letter or report. Don't hesitate to start over if you can remove the sexism from your writing by doing so. It is worth the effort to make certain you are not excluding or insulting any of your readers.

Changing the pronoun to first or second person, for instance, could entail an entire rewriting job. The decision to change the subjects to plurals will also require much rewriting to be sure you are changing the verbs to agree. There will be times when you need to step back and ask yourself, just what am I trying to say here and how can I do it without excluding half the population?

The following paragraph needs to be rewritten entirely. To try to patch or substitute words would only confuse the issue. In the interest of clear and accurate writing, this one needs a new beginning. See how much better it scans with the rewrite.

S: Every time a farmer takes his hay to market, he finds that not only have prices changed, but the rules have changed as well. His predicament is compounded by his use of outdated equipment, vehicles he bought when he started farming many years ago.

N: The plight of today's farmer is complicated. Prices change from day to day; rules change rapidly as well. In addition, many farmers use vehicles purchased many years ago when they began farming.

In the above rewrite, the subject was changed from *a farmer* to *the plight of today's farmer,* thus emphasizing that plight. A much stronger statement evolves.

An easier way to rewrite is to include a modifying phrase or clause to take care of exclusive pronouns.

Example:

S: If a reader needs a good book, he goes to the library.

N: A reader who needs a good book goes to the library.

USE SINGULAR NOUNS THAT TAKE PLURAL PRONOUNS

Shakespeare did it. So did George Bernard Shaw, F. Scott Fitzgerald, and many more of the world's great authors. They used singular antecedents with plural pronouns. One dictionary includes in its definition of *their* "used with an indefinite third person singular antecedent," citing W.H. Auden's "anyone in their senses."

Today's language is considerably different from the language of our ancestors, simply because language changes and develops as people's use of it changes and develops. If you need proof, leaf through an old dictionary and see how words and their meanings change.

An obvious example of changing language is the elimination of formal second-person pronouns: *thee, thy,* and *thou.* Another example of usage adaptation is the *you-all* that is accepted in some parts of the country as the plural form of *you.*

There was a time when grammar teachers placed large red marks on school papers that contained such sentences as "Every ball player should have their own mitt." or "Any student can write their own essay."

Now, thanks to many recognized language authorities, some grammarians are accepting the plural pronoun with the singular antecedent. Strong precedents have been established to use the pronouns *they, their,* and *them* following the use of such words as *every, each, any,* and *some,* as well as after any singular antecedent of undetermined or inclusive gender.

However, there still is substantial controversy over this stretching of our language. Old-school holdouts argue that to use plural pronouns with singular antecedents presents confusion, an area open to misunderstanding. And many times they are right. In certain circumstances, this usage will indeed be inaccurate. In that case, you may wish to use the compound *he or she* (see "The Last-Ditch Effort").

Example:

Each participant is responsible only for their own materials.

Much clearer:
Each participant is responsible only for his or her own materials.

Less awkward:
Participants are responsible only for their own materials.

The following would be smiled upon by Mr. Shakespeare, et al.:

Each one attending should have their own notebook.
Anyone can present their ideas in public.
Everyone can name their own price.
Someone has provided more than their share.

THE LAST-DITCH EFFORT

Earlier it was observed that language rules follow usage and not the other way around. Language is put to use before it appears in dictionaries. Sometimes we believe that language can be forced into usage, but this seldom works. (Remember Esperanto? It was conceived in an attempt to form a universal language that everyone, all humans around the world, could speak. It never took hold.)

When the problem of sexism began to seriously bother people, attempts were made to come up with a nonsexist third-person pronoun (other than *it*). This hasn't worked either, mostly because the solutions offered weren't pronounceable or were so obscure they were unknown to most of us.

Occasionally in writing, as a last-ditch effort to salvage a sentence from sexism, multiple pronouns can be used. But, please, only as a last-ditch effort!

Examples:
A mechanic must conduct business according to his or her own standards.

Often seen, but less desirable, constructions might include:
The attitudes of a business owner are reflected in his/her employees.

or:
Whether or not a barber is successful depends upon the way (s)he treats the customer.

Ultimately, we're left with a few general rules for handling sexist-pronoun situations: make the pronouns plural, replace them, eliminate them, or rewrite to get around them.

5 Sexism by Endings and Implication

Many words express sexist gender by endings other than *man* (Chapter 3). The main culprits are word endings derived through assimilation of words from other languages into English usage. These endings contribute much to sexist language.

Why should we care about the endings of words and the effect of endings on sexism? Mostly because identification of roles and people by word endings is discriminatory due to their inconsistent application. If our language used endings to identify linguistic gender (as do Romance languages), there would be no problem. In countries with Latin-based languages, noun and adjective endings function as a major component of the language. In English, we do not distinguish adjectives and nouns by gender. However, we do borrow some endings from other languages to differentiate certain roles and positions.

Latin, which forms the base for much of English, is a language that provides gender identity to all nouns, in a way that doesn't always make much sense. For instance, the Latin word for *sailor* is *nauta* (feminine), and the word for *farmer* is *agricola* (feminine). That doesn't mean that Latin sailors and farmers were women; it means the words were given feminine gender for linguistic purposes. This language quirk persists in all Romance languages (such as Spanish, Italian, French, and Portuguese) and in one form or another in many other languages—all of which adds to the confusion.

Unfortunately, some of the masculine and feminine endings have been perpetuated in our language. Words like *alumnus* and *alumna* have been so incorporated into English that the original Latin gender endings exist even though they are often unused (except by academia). Correct usage (in Latin) is *alumnus, alumni* (masculine singular and plural) and *alumna, alumnae* (feminine singular and plural), which makes *Dear Alumnus* translate to *Dear Sir*, thus excluding women graduates. It also makes *Dear Alumnas* technically incorrect. The current and increasing tendency in popular usage, however, is to pluralize *alumna* by adding an *s* rather than the Latin *e*. (Apologies to Latin purists.)

The French indicate feminine nouns by adding an *e* to otherwise masculine nouns, implying that the masculine is the norm and the "altered" word applies to the feminine. Other French endings that feminize the norm are *euse, ette, enne,* and *ess*.

Examples:
blond (*masculine*), blonde (*feminine*)
fiancé (*masculine*), fianceé (*feminine*)
masseur (*masculine*), masseuse (*feminine*)
comedian (*masculine*), comedienne (*feminine*)

This has led to the American habit of making two forms of many nouns—one masculine, the other feminine—when only one noun is required.

Examples:
Usher, usherette; major, majorette; author, authoress; adulterer, adulteress; conductor, conductress; heir, heiress; shepherd, shepherdess; god, goddess.

Ask yourself whether there is a question as to the gender of the following people: seamstress, song-stress, waitress, and actress. The jobs of these people could be accurately defined in a nonsexist manner with the terms *sewer, singer, waiter,* and *actor.*

Another language carry-over from Latin is the use of the suffix *ix* to change the male *executor* into the female *executrix,* or *aviator* into *aviatrix.* Actually, either a man or woman can handle an executor's job or an aviator's work.

Note that in all of these spelling changes, the masculine is considered the root word, or norm. The feminine form, built upon that, is the afterthought, the addition. Therefore, by qualifying a noun with *ess, euse, ette, ix,* or any such endings, the male by implication represents the standard and the female is the deviation. Discrimination by endings can be overcome simply by using sexually neutral words, such as

> *heir, poet, laundry worker, singer, author, waiter, shepherd, farmer, comedian, executor,* and *adulterer* (whether male or female).

Sex should not be used as a basis to differentiate between two qualified people. The law backs this up. A licensed pilot is an aviator; a licensed physician is a doctor; a poet is a poet; an author is an author.

Discrimination by implication is another matter, not so easily cured by changing the endings. Many words have been given sexist meanings because of long-term stereotyped usage. Because secretaries and nurses historically have been women, the words imply femininity; because most attorneys and doctors have been men, the words imply masculinity. In the interest of accuracy, these discriminating tendencies just don't apply anymore. However, the implications linger on.

The use of euphemisms is another source of sexist implication in language. "Women's work" has fallen largely into the low-paying or nonpaying jobs, which include secretaries, clerks, waiters, nurses, teachers, tellers, and volunteers. But consider the masculine image that accompanies such high-paying professions as lawyer, CEO, executive, doctor, professor, banker, and superintendent. The use of euphemisms may seem to distract or hide the implied meanings, but consider:

> Administrative Assistant (secretary)
> Domestic Engineer (housewife)
> Sanitary Engineer (janitor)
> Customer Service Representative (clerk/teller)

Euphemisms seem to appear readily for the low-paying or nonpaying jobs, but they appear less readily for *doctor, professor,* or *banker.*

You can reduce sexism in your environment and remove it from your writing by referring to job categories and professions by their accurate terms. Don't fall for the euphemisms that may mask an economic deficiency with a fancy title. If in doubt, consult the Glossary of Alternative Terms at the back of this book.

6 Words That Diminish or Demean

What is the difference between a chef and a cook? Which is the man? Which is the woman? Give yourself 10 points if you couldn't distinguish. Go to the front of the book if you identified the chef as a man and the cook as a woman.

Many words, like *chef* and *cook*, have sexist connotations. When prestige is involved, it tends to go to the masculine-sounding word. Too many words are used to diminish the importance of women and to demean their identities.

GIRL/GAL

According to biological definition, a girl is a feminine human who has not reached puberty. *Gal* is just another way to say *girl*. Both terms apply to females up to the age of mid- or late teens. Generally, girls become women (or young women) about the age of 14. Both *girl* and *gal* are demeaning when applied to adult women, whether or not it often is thought "cute" to refer to older women as such.

Likewise, a boy is a masculine human who has not reached puberty. Consider how demeaning is the term *boy* when referring to a man.

If both sexes of people of similar age are referred to as *girls* and *boys*, the terms may be acceptable. The discrimination occurs when boys of a particular age are referred to as *men*, while the girls are still *girls*.

The following teams are made up of young people under the age of 14. Yet, we read: "The men's basketball team won by 6 points; the girls' team won by 17."

MANHOOD/WOMANHOOD

The state of being a man or a woman is referred to as *manhood* or *womanhood*. While the word structure is similar, the connotations are not.

Perhaps the clearest indication of the difference is found in a negative reference, as in "a threat to his manhood," compared to "a threat to her womanhood." Somehow, men consider a threat more serious than women.

Visualize a man in a skirt. What this does to threaten his manhood can be seen by the reactions of other men. Most are aghast that a man would think so little of his manhood that he would don women's clothing.

Now visualize a woman in trousers. This doesn't seem to threaten a woman's womanhood—at least not in the same way. Most women don slacks often these days and no one thinks much about it. So why is this single activity so demeaning to men and of little concern to women?

Whatever the reason, there are words that do the same damage to manhood as wearing a skirt. These are the words that question the virility of a man, that question his "really being a man." And those words begin with *sissy* in childhood and grow to *effeminate, lightweight,* or *like a girl* in adulthood. They are fighting words to most men, words deserving of even physical defense of one's manhood.

Conversely, women don't take the same kind of offense at being referred to as masculine. In some instances, they consider it a compliment. Even words that describe or insinuate a woman's sexual preference, like *lesbian*, don't bring out deep-seated anger in most women.

In an episode of the sitcom "The Cosby Show," Dr. Huxtable surveys a plumbing repair job and comments to the plumber (a woman), "That looks like a two-man job." To which she replies, "It could be a two-man job. Or it could be a one-woman job." Whose *-hood* was more wounded, hers at being patronized as not being able to conduct her work properly or his at being told one woman could handle a job that otherwise might take two men?

TOMBOY/SISSY

Children begin to get word messages about their sexual identities long before they know who they are. Use of words like *tomboy* or *sissy* to youngsters confuses their self-perception and sense of sexual identity. Children have a rough enough time trying to learn who they are without having to overcome such words of derision.

When referring to a girl who is active, use words like *strong, vigorous, adventurous, spirited, competitive,* and *self-confident.* But do not use *tomboy.*

The word *sissy* applied to a boy is a put-down. It even denotes a put-down when applied to a girl. If a boy is sensitive, use words like *quiet, perceptive, understanding, caring, artistic, introspective, gentle, modest,* and *peaceful.* But don't use *sissy.*

WOMEN AS THINGS

Accurate use of words identifies people with gender terms and inanimate things with the pronoun *it*. Find the precise word to delineate the thing itself. Save gender words for people, and then only if they apply. A man is properly referred to with masculine pronouns and possessive adjectives: *he, him,* and *his*; and a woman is properly referred to by feminine pronouns and possessive adjectives: *she, her,* and *hers*.

Personification of boats, autos, hurricanes, machines, and so on as sexual beings is both incongruent and inaccurate. Avoid such terms as "give her the gas," or "she's a real twister this time!" or "the mechanic should have her ready in a half-hour."

Conversely, avoid using terms of things for people. Do not refer to a woman as *cookie, sugar, honey,* a *dish,* a *tomato,* a *doll,* a *clinging vine,* a *wallflower,* or a *fashion plate.* Do you realize that nuclear power plants are referred to as "sister plants," or that elements of radioactive decay are referred to as "element's daughters"? These terms are demeaning to women, particularly in light of women's efforts toward peacemaking.

Just a few words about *dear.* When a man calls a woman to whom he is not closely related "dear," the term is insulting. Some men (especially older ones) enjoy using this term with women, justifying it by calling the term "friendly." However, these men would be unlikely to use *dear* with other men to be "friendly," and that is what makes it discriminatory and demeaning.

Women who use similar terms with men they don't know (or hardly know) are using the same demeaning process. Some think that a woman clerk or waiter who uses terms like "honey" or "dear" is attempting to put herself on a more equal footing with the man she is waiting on. This idea points strongly to the method of using endearing terms with strangers as a way of reducing their power—male or female.

WOMEN AS ENTITIES

Define women by who they are, not by who their fathers or husbands are or by their children or grandchildren. Women do things besides get married and have children and should be recognized for all of their accomplishments.

Whether or not a woman prefers to use *Mrs., Miss,* or *Ms.,* her first name should be used only as often as men use the first names of other men. Too often women address men they deal with as "Mr. So-and-So" while men address the women they deal with by their first names. Notice how often women address professional men as *Mr.* or *Dr.* while hearing themselves addressed as "Betty," "Ann," or, even worse, "Sweetheart" or "Dear"!

When writing to or talking to women, don't use "Mrs. Ben Adams." She would be better referred to with her own name, "Betty Adams," "Mrs. Betty Adams," or "Ms. Betty Adams." To decide which to use, learn her preference. You may also ask yourself if this reference would be appropriate if used for a man. Mr. Ben Adams most likely would not stand still for being called "Mr. Betty Adams." If you don't know the woman's preferred title, use a respectful one, as you would in addressing a man you didn't know well.

Regarding the use of reference to one's children (or other household associations), ask yourself whether it would make sense to use the reference to children with the other sex. A woman is more than a "housewife," "grandmother," or "mother of three."

In a news item, is the subject identified by the role played in the news story? Or is the subject identified by personal roles and descriptions?

Examples:

The juror is a mother of three children. (Only if another juror is identified as *the father of two.*)

Margaret Thompson has been a member of the Board of Directors for six years. *She is the wife (mother or grandmother) of* . . . . (Only if you similarly would say: Marvin Thompson has been a member of the Board of Directors for six years. *He is the husband (father or grandfather) of* . . . .)

WIFE

A wife is a woman married to a man. The opposite of *wife* is *husband*. One does not own or supersede the other. It is inaccurate to use *man and wife*. Rather, use *husband and wife* or *woman and man*. There is no prescribed order; either word could be used first.

Use of certain words with *wife* often identifies a woman as an appendage or chattel. Avoid such degrading terms as *the wife, my wife, the little woman, my better half, the ball and chain*, and *just a wife*. When two people marry, one does not become the property of the other; one does not belong to the other. Likewise, two married people do not become *one*, implying two half-people. Two married people become two people sharing their lives.

And watch out for implications of tagging along with a spouse, such as *faculty wife, corporate wife,* senate wife, and *neighbor's wife.* The neighbor or senator may object to the reference to *her* spouse as a wife.

LADY

The term *lady* is difficult to define because of many current usage connotations. In most cases, the word evokes standards of propriety and elegance, such as in *first lady* and *leading lady.* In others, a definition of *lady* refers to her behavior, as with a *lady of the evening* or *lady in waiting. Lady* has been defined as "slangy, pompous, presumptuous, and patronizing," depending on the tone of voice.

Other times, the word indicates diminution, as in *cleaning lady, saleslady,* and *forelady.* These are condescending subterms for *janitor, salesman,* and *foreman,* and they imply that women doing these jobs are female forms of the *original*; thus the terms are uncomplimentary.

The jury is still out as to the meaning of the possessive *my lady,* when referring to a female friend. Even when it is said with stars in the man's eyes, the term has undertones of possessiveness in it.

A submeaning for the use of *lady* is the gratuitous adjective to a noun: *lady doctor, lady's tool kit.* What's wrong with simply *doctor* or *tool kit?* Another term with submeaning is *lady of the house.* This is close to a patronizing term to make the woman feel important and put her in a mood to be sold something. Put-downs occur when *lady* is used to identify the gender of a person behind a job title or other label. When tempted to use *lady attorney, lady doctor,* or *lady driver*, forget the sex-referenced adjective and stick to the noun label.

Examples:

S: The lady lawyer and the young attorney had lunch.

N: The two lawyers had lunch.

S: Surgery was performed by the lady doctor.

N: Surgery was performed by the doctor.

While you're avoiding *lady doctor*, keep away from *male nurse*, *male secretary*, and *male teacher*. Sexism in language occurs with both sexes.

If identification by gender is really necessary, once is enough in a news article or report. And the words should be *woman* or *man*, as in *woman prime minister*, *woman judge*, *man secretary*, or *man agent*. Even then, make the distinction only if it is pertinent.

DO'S AND DON'TS

Stay away from such phrases as *greatest woman golfer of the club* and *darn good for a woman!* These are condescending and demeaning terms.

Order of placement also can imply second-class citizenship or second place. When terms are used continually, as with *man and woman*, *husband and wife*, *his and hers*, and *fathers and mothers*, the subliminal message of men first, women second is repeated. Vary the order in your writing and usage and change the stereotyped wording.

Observe parallel treatment of terms:
Women and men (adults)
Boys and girls (children)

Parenthetical inclusion of women also is insulting. Rewrite if necessary, but avoid the afterthought implication found in such terminology as:

S: All company men (and women) are invited.
The rules apply to all boys (and girls) under
10.

N: All company women and men are invited.
The rules apply to all boys and girls under
10.

or:

All company employees are invited.
The rules apply to all children under 10.

Take time to consider usage of terms referring to
women, and give thought to how similar terms are
used when referring to men. All women are created
equal (and men, too)!

7 Mind Your Nonsexist Business

Just as styles of business management change with the times, so do styles of business writing. As more and more women enter the work force, business management and styles of writing are being updated—in keeping with the times.

Smart business people recognize the biological fact that (at least) half the population is composed of women. It would follow that (at least) half of the consumers are women, women who need to be sold on a product or service if it is to gain maximum returns for the company. Likewise, business is noticing more women in all fields joining the ranks of ownership, supervisory management, sales forces, and mid-management. Each year the numbers of what used to be termed "men's" jobs are diminishing.

Acknowledging the influx of women both as consumers and as business participants, business language is being modified in both form and content to avoid sexism in business correspondence. Some of the old rules are being changed.

CONTRACTS

Not only are some fields of industry scrambling to clear up their contractual agreements, but they are also using the idea as a marketing tool to attract customers. Insurance companies and automobile dealers alike are working to simplify contracts.

Still, many contracts include somewhere in the glossary of terms or preamble to the agreement a little clause that states in so many words, ". . . the masculine shall include the feminine and the neuter." Somehow this disclaimer seems to say that it will take care of everything that those who drafted the contract didn't have the time or energy or inclination to care about. The language disclaimer is reminiscent of the clauses that appeared in 18th-century documents about rights that "accrue to all men, excluding prisoners, the insane, slaves, women, and children."

An easier way to solve the problem of which gender to use in a contract that may apply to either women or men is to go through the contract and change all the third-person pronouns to genderless terms, using any or all of the suggestions regarding pronouns found in Chapter 4.

How much more pleasant and equitable to refer to the party of the first part as the seller, mortgagor, lender, corporation, or contractor and the party of the second part as the buyer, mortgagee, borrower, private party, or contractee! Or, how about Party I and Party II?

LETTERS/CORRESPONDENCE

Changes occur in different ways for different reasons. When electric typewriters began to appear in offices, for instance, the form of business letters began to change. Ease of typing letters without indented paragraphs, datelines, and closings produced the block form of letter. Business was not adversely affected; in fact, business letters using the block form are strikingly neat and easy to read.

Yet many of these letters still begin and end with archaic phrases that can be called "terms of endearment." Still heading many business letters are the archaic salutations *Dear Sir* (even though the address-ee is not identified as a sir) and *Gentlemen* (even though the addressee is known to be a company, not necessarily a group of men).

Even more archaic and useless are the closings still found in business letters. Busy people could save countless hours by omitting the senseless closings on letters. Think how much time you would save if you didn't have to decide whether you were *sincere, cordial, true,* or *very true.* These terms are meaningless and just take up space that could better be used to close with an action-producing message.

Modern business writers have discovered a variety of nonsexist methods for starting a letter written to a company or to an unidentified person. Choose the method that best suits the situation of the letter: omit the salutation, use a reference line, use a department name or department-head title, or start your answer in the salutation. (See also Habits Are Hard to Break, Chapter 8.)

Omit the Salutation

Business people are busy people. By trimming a letter of the decorative endearments (the opening *dear* and the closing *very truly yours, sincerely,* or other such cozy extras), the business message is made more clear.

There is nothing sacred about these terms. Not too many years ago, business people felt it necessary to close their letters with such fanciful terms as *Trusting to be favored by your further orders, We are, Gentlemen, And remain,* and *Yours faithfully.* This unnatural language of business went out of style long ago. Today's business writers are concise while remaining courteous.

Omit the salutation (and likewise the closing) if you are unsure as to the identity of the addressee. Use the *Dear Sir* only if you have addressed the letter to a male person and wish to retain the very formal tone.

Use a Reference Line

Starting a letter with the opening sentence may be a bit too brisk for you. If something seems to belong between the address and the first paragraph, try a reference line. Give the reader a head start in learning the reason for the letter.

Examples:

Re: Order No. 1234, shipped June 1
Re: Invitation to Speak March 12
Re: Request for credit data
Re: Account No. 5678

Use the reference line when you are dealing with account numbers, case or file numbers, purchase orders, or policy numbers. When a letter is not addressed to a single person or department, someone has to read it, determine its destination, and route it for handling. When you state the purpose of the letter and case numbers in the opening line, the mail router will know exactly who should receive the letter.

Use a Department Name

You know the purpose of your letter and therefore the department that should receive it. If you do not know the name of the specific person your letter will reach, use the department name in your reference line. Even if you are unsure of the correct department title, your definition will direct the letter sorter to see that the letter gets to the right place.

Examples:

To: The Order Department
To: The Catalog Department
To: The Mail Order Department

Use a Department-Head Title

Similarly, if you don't have a person's name, you usually can decide on the title that would best fit.

Examples:

Attn: Customer Complaint Director
Attn: Customer Service Manager
Attn: Computer Equipment Repairs Manager

Start Your Answer, My Friend

And get right into the letter. This is where your imagination and creativity can take over. You can be as warm and friendly as you wish or as firm and friendly as you wish. Your message can be carefully constructed to do just the job you want it to.

Examples:

Good morning, Joshua,
Here is the information I promised to send when we talked on the phone yesterday.

Yes, Marge,
your order went out on Monday, just as I thought. You'll be receiving it in a few days.

No, Terry,
Your order will not be shipped until we have
received full payment for the last order you
received.

You have my promise, Emma,
You and I will meet for an interview as soon as I
have completed the work on the job description.

Closings

When omitting the standard ho-hum salutation, there
is little need to clutter up a business letter with the use
of a moldy closing. A typist can leave space for a signature and type in the writer's name. In this way, you
can let your final remark make its full impact without
obstructing the message with archaic words.

Examples:

Please let me know your decision before the
end of the month.

A. B. Carson, President

Take advantage of this time-saving offer while
this discount is still effective.

Marty Jones
Marketing Director

If you feel absolutely compelled to use some kind of
make-nice closing, a simple *Sincerely* should do the
job.

A note about signatures in business. Courtesy titles
(*Mr.* and *Ms.*) are omitted in the signature block
unless there is a special reason. Occasionally, if a writer wishes to identify the gender of a name that could

be either male or female, the identifying courtesy title is typed in parentheses.

Example:

L. G. Anderson,
President

or
(Ms.) L. G. Anderson,
President

Unless there is a reason to disclose the marital status of the female writer, the courtesy titles of *Miss* and *Mrs.* are not used in nonsexist business writing.

In short, use only the courtesy titles *Ms.* and *Mr.* for all business people. If you wish, ask the woman how she prefers to be addressed. And if you use *Mrs.*, use the first name of the woman instead of her husband's first name.

SEXISM CAN COST YOU DOLLARS

Business-letter writing has been elevated to an art of coming to the point succinctly and courteously. With the influx of paper moving through most modern offices, and with time at more of a premium, recipients of such clear and concise letters appreciate the timesaving consideration that results in saved money. At the same time these letters are much easier to write.

All the other rules of writing nonsexist language apply to the contents of such letters. Care must be taken to avoid undue reference to *businessmen, your secretary . . . she, the office manager . . . he,* or the *salesmen* in the company.

Women who hold responsible jobs with a company may lose valuable work hours when they are treated as less than valuable to the company. When a woman manager is constantly referred to as *the girl in charge of . . .*, she may begin to question her own worth. Indecision and concern over status within the company can cause lost time—and therefore lost money—to the business.

Address women in business by their names and titles in the same way you would address men in their positions.

ADVERTISING CAN BE A TURN-OFF

Company advertising is another place where sexist language can cost a business precious dollars. Recently a furniture company sent out a flier offering gift ideas: *a reclining chair for HIM* and *a cedar chest for HER*. The implications, clearly sexist, probably lost sales for the company from women who wanted recliners (or men who wanted cedar chests).

An automobile company is "proud to offer discounts to our valuable customers. The customer is *king* at our auto agency. *He* is treated to the best in service and quality products." Too bad! The company isn't catching the attention of the many women who don't enjoy being treated as kings and who don't appreciate being referred to as "he."

Clearly, many businesses that sell high-ticket items are missing sales because they overlook women as potential customers. More and more women are in the market for new cars, houses, airplanes, computers, boats, sports equipment, and furniture.

Advertising copy that automatically relegates women to the housekeeper role and men to the protector/provider role is no longer acceptable to many potential customers. Don't risk losing half of your potential buyers by turning them off with sexist language. It simply is not good business.

If you are doing direct-mail business, be careful of the means of addressing your potential customers. Generic terms like *Dear Customer, Dear Householder,* and *Dear Driver* will successfully reach anyone, man or woman, who may come in to buy your product or service. But terms like *Dear Housewife, Dear Fisherman,* and *Dear Businessman* may just be an annoyance to the person opening the mail.

Here are some more nonsexist terms you may wish to consider: *owner, leader, executive, helper, artist, assistant, developer, creator, analyst, clerk, speaker, representative, builder, manager,* and *advertiser.*

AFFIRMATIVE ACTION

Besides all the dollars-and-cents reasons for using nonsexist language in your business, there are some legal aspects. Treating employees differently according to their sex is clearly against the law and could result in unrest (at best) and lawsuits (at worst).

Most businesses are top-heavy with male decision-makers, while women are clustered about the lower-paying jobs. Have you considered the role these women play in the operation of the business? Usually they are the ones who have direct contact with your customers. They are the secretaries, clerks, nurses, teachers, bookkeepers, and tellers.

If you want a clear-cut view of your office as it pertains to affirmative action and treatment of women and men, ask yourself (whether you are male or female) how your mother, sister, daughter, or best woman friend would feel working in your office.

BUSINESS ASSOCIATES

Another area that can lose profit dollars to a business is the way business associates are treated.

More and more supply companies are run by women, and to assume that such businesses are men-owned may be erroneous and certainly is costly. At the same time, the chances are greater that to do business with another company will require dealing with a woman in a decision-making position. Inability to deal with executive women as equals is likely to result in more lost business.

Women still have a long way to go in the world of business, but they are moving fast—faster than at any previous time. Although their average earnings still are considerably less than those of men, women are filling more responsible roles and achieving greater success in operating their own businesses. As these changes occur, the need to recognize women as a valuable part of the business world can be achieved through adherence to nonsexist, inclusive language.

8 Habits Are Hard To Break

Many of the linguistic habits in use today have been deeply ingrained by centuries of repetition. Cultural use has determined other habits. All are difficult to break—but not impossible.

Take salutations, for instance. Business instructors have begun to recognize the uselessness of the salutation on most letters. Business letters in greater numbers are appearing on desks without the formerly sacred *Dear Sir or Madam.* Sometimes a reference line serves the same introductory purpose, as in *To the Sales Manager* or *Re: Sales Department.*

When the addressee is unidentified, the reference line is adequate. When addressing named persons, use just the name and title.

Examples:

Dear Mary Doe,

Dear Dr. Doe,

Dear Professor Doe (the title is spelled out for such titles as *Senator, Justice, Governor, Professor,* and *President*)

Dear Ms. Doe,

Dear Pat Smith,

Dear Chris Olson,

The same treatment applies to addressing anyone, man or woman—just the name and title.

Some businesses address mail to the recipient according to role or relationship to business:

Dear Homeowner,
Dear Reader,
Dear Parent, (and please, not *Mom*)

WRITING TO MEMBERS OF CONGRESS

Have you noticed that some of our *Congressmen* are women?

When writing to your Congressional Representative, be sure you find the appropriate title to use. The correct title for a member of the Senate is *Senator*. A member of the other legislative branch is a *Member of the House*, a *Congressional Representative*, or a *Member of Congress*. Read through the Constitution of the United States and you will not find any of these representatives called Congressman. What better authority for you to follow?

FIRST NAMES

When writing a news story or a write-up about people, use the first name of the individual only if first names are used for everyone; otherwise use last names and titles. It is belittling to call a woman by her first name while using the title and last name for a man. Consistency is the guideline.

Do not use:
President and Bess Truman

Use:
President Truman and Mrs. Truman

or
Harry and Bess Truman

Use:
Governor Evans and Governor Ray

but not
Governor Evans and Dixie Lee Ray

If both marital partners share titles (as with doctors), their titles should be used equally: *Dr. Doe and Dr. Doe,* or *the Drs. Doe* (not *Dr. and Mrs. Doe,* or *Dr. and Mr. Doe*).

MASCULINE/FEMININE

Traits and qualities of humans are found in both sexes. *Strong* and *brave* do not necessarily mean "masculine," nor are *tender* and *nurturing* automatically feminine traits. Beware of the temptation to use sex-linked adjectives to describe characteristics shared by all humans. When inclined to use a feminine or masculine symbol, look for a better image—inclusive rather than stereotypical, a symbol that *includes* rather than stereotypes.

Avoid the trap of giving inanimate things gender. Implications of unpredictability or treachery that accompany such words as *witch, Mother Nature, mother of change,* and *weak sex* give unfair meanings to femininity. Likewise, words like *master, father,* and *patron* cast implied masculine meanings of leadership and power. Be aware of the habitual use of these and similar terms and the context in which they are used.

Unfortunately, dictionaries contribute to the misuse of many adjectives. One defines *female* as an adjective meaning "womanish, or unmanly." *Male,* on the other hand, is never defined as being "mannish, or unwomanly."

PATRON

The word *patron*, from the Latin word *pater* ("father"), means "benefactor or protector." When you use this word to confer the meaning of *benefactor*, you imply the fatherly connotation. Instead, use such words as *sponsor, donor*, or *supporter*.

In the same manner, a patronizing remark is one that condescends (in a fatherly, authoritarian, protective way).

PERSON

The average person on the street is not necessarily a man. Since half the population are women (actually slightly more than half), avoid using such terms as "man on the street" unless you are referring to a specific man on the street. It is just as easy to talk about "people on the street," a "person on the street," an "average person," or a "typical person."

In the same way, hypothetical people are not always men. Textbooks are beginning to use inclusive language to present math and other problems and examples.

Example:

S: If a man can jog three miles an hour, how long would it take him to jog six miles?

N: If a jogger can run three miles an hour, how long would it take to jog six miles?

WARNING: Avoid the overuse of the word *person*. So many specific and accurate words are available that inserting *person* whenever you are confused about gender becomes unnecessary. Neither is it necessary to use *person* when you really mean a man.

If you are talking about a man in sales, by all means use the term *salesman.* But if you are talking about some unidentified person in sales, use *person.* You can also use such specific words as *clerk, agent, representative,* or any number of accurate nouns.

Be sure that when you use *person,* it is to refer to an unidentified or nongender-specific individual. Don't use *spokesman,* for instance, in reference to a man, then *spokesperson* to refer to a woman doing the same job. In that instance, she is the *spokeswoman.*

Person need be neither ridiculously overused nor overzealously avoided.

SPORTS

All baseball players are not men—nor are all athletic figures and sports players men. Sports is not an exclusively male domain. Use either *male baseball players* or *female baseball players* when specifying certain gender-restricted players, or just use *baseball players* when referring to people who play baseball.

If you refer to sports people as either *Mr.* or *Ms.* for identification, do so equally for both men and women.

Example:

S: Ms. Lloyd and O'Connor played in a mixed double.

N: Ms. Lloyd and Mr. O'Connor played in a mixed double.

or

Lloyd and O'Connor played in a mixed double.

ANIMALS

As long as we personify animals in cartoons, advertisements, and stories, we need to recognize the biological fact that all animals are not male, nor are all animals female.

While this may seem obvious, popular usage seems to give male gender to the birds of the air, animals of the woods, and fish in the sea. Some of these habits have caused some ludicrous and inaccurate sentences like the following:

> The cow had a fly on *his* tail.
> The doe had a frightened look in *his* eye.
> The two-year-old mare won *his* first race by six lengths.

Do not assume that an animal is male unless the word (such as *buck*) makes this clear or the animal's sex is otherwise specified. Too many textbooks, as well as story books, abound with such statements as these:

> The white-tailed deer lives in his woodland habitat.
> The turtle's shell is his home.
> When a seagull searches for his dinner . . . .
> All of the pig is used commercially, even his tail.

In the English language, it is perfectly right to refer to animals with the neuter gender pronoun *it*. Remember, the deer in the forest, rabbits under the trees, chickens in the yard, and dogs in the pound all share sexual distinctions. All species come in two genders, female and male. Use *he* when referring to male animals, *she* for female animals, and *it* when you don't know the animal's sex or when it is unimportant.

Animal terms, when applied to people, can demean through sexual implication, as in *bull session* or *hen party*. It is unlikely you can avoid all such terms, but at least be aware of how they are used. And be aware of the effect on those receiving the innuendoes.

WOMEN AT WORK

The traditional role of woman as homemaker and principal parent has set up habitual usage that requires attention. For too many years, the homemaker has been referred to as "just a housewife" or a "nonworking woman." Both usages are inaccurate. Homemakers, both male and female, work—sometimes harder than anyone else. They just don't receive a paycheck. Likewise, homemakers are doing important work and should not be referred to with the diminishing *just*.

Do you assume that women are responsible for operating the home? If so, you may need to take a closer look at what is happening around you. Some homes are being operated by "househusbands." Take care when sending a note home with a youngster that you don't address it to *Mom*. Or when you want the chief homemaker, don't assume this will be the *lady of the house*.

A *working wife* is a married woman whose arms and legs move! Too many people still identify women as *working* wives, mothers, or housewives. Such definitions are condescending and should be avoided. Men are seldom identified as *working husbands, fathers*, or *just husbands*.

Women who hold salaried jobs are *business-women, sales representatives, salaried women, administrators*, or any number of other such job titles. The woman who holds a job at home (paid or unpaid) is a *woman who works at home*.

Take care with terms like *motherhood, fatherhood, parenting, homemaking, wife, husband, grandmother,* and *grandfather*. Are you using them accurately and appropriately? Both societal roles and word usage are changing. If one candidate is referred to as a "grandmother of six," then another might be described as a "grandfather of four."

NOTE: Isn't it strange that job categories are divided into "men's work" and "nontraditional work"? If you want to realize just how strange, consider "women's work" as opposed to "nontraditional work."

SEX ROLES

People sometimes are expected to assume roles in life according to their gender, rather than according to their abilities and desires as individuals.

The roles we are expected to assume begin when we are children. Girls grow up playing with dolls and learning roles that are passive, accommodating, and nurturing—housekeeper, wife, mother, and generally submissive human being. Boys, on the other hand, grow up with baseball bats, trucks, and scooters, learning roles that are active and commanding—father, protector, wage-earner, and generally aggressive human being.

Psychology researchers are discovering that these tendencies are learned, that we teach girls to prepare for submissive roles by keeping them quiet as youngsters. At the same time, we teach boys to prepare for aggressive roles by keeping them active as children. What if we give girls a rough-and-tumble childhood and boys a relaxing, inactive childhood? Would their adult roles be different than they are now? You bet, say many researchers.

Toymakers are busy designing toys for *children*, toys that are equally attractive to boys and girls, whether they are active or inactive children. Parents are debating the pros and cons of giving trains and basketballs to girls, dolls and tea sets to boys.

Meanwhile, children grow up hearing and reading stories about males, such as Peter Rabbit and Father Time. They observe holidays at school by coloring pictures of Santa Claus, Tom Turkey, St. Patrick, St. Valentine, and even Snoopy (boy dog)—all male figures.

Heroes of our nation are depicted as men, beginning with George Washington, Father of Our Country, and moving forward. Dictionaries even define *hero* as "1) a man of distinguished courage or ability, admired for his brave deeds. 2) a man who is regarded as having heroic qualities. 3) the principal male character in a story, play, etc. 4) a man of great strength and courage, favored by the gods and in part descended from them, often regarded as a half-god and worshiped after his death." Where does that leave women? With *heroine*, a "girl or woman of outstanding courage, nobility, etc., or of heroic achievements." In other words, a female who acts bravely, *like a (male) hero.* (An ironic note: The word *hero* comes from the Greek priestess of Aphrodite named Hero, the woman who loved Leander. When Leander was drowned trying to swim the Hellespont to be with her, Hero threw herself into the sea.)

FOUNDING FATHERS, BROTHERS, AND BOMFOG

This country's pioneers, founders, trailblazers, and innovators were not all men. Writers of history need to include women in the wording and connotations of those who came before. *Founding fathers* can be changed easily to *forebears*. Pioneers usually are defined in masculine terms, when the facts clearly show that many pioneers were women.

Even further back, our predecessors are presented to us as *cavemen*. We talk about *Piltdown Man, Neanderthal Man, Cro-Magnon Man*, and so on. Biologically, we know there had to be cavewomen or we wouldn't be here now. Curiously, the proof of these cave people turned up in the form of bone remains that were identified as belonging to cavewomen.

Brotherhood is another word that cannot accurately include women. The word *kindred* better expresses this idea; it includes both women and men. *Siblinghood* might be stretching too far.

BOMFOG is translated to stand for "Brotherhood Of Man/Fatherhood Of God," a term that sounds very noble until you think about all the people who are left out.

SUBLIMINAL MESSAGES

Another way that sexist language crops up is through the subliminal meanings of certain cultural attitudes. The attitudes that women are passive and men are active are based on beliefs that certain words are more powerful than others.

Women may refer to a color as *mauve*; men will tend to call it *purple*. Women use adjectives like *little, really*, and *somewhat*, whereas men tend to avoid these detracting words. Women use more passive language; men seem to use more direct terminology.

Women don't always take themselves or their work seriously. Some women downplay activities by referring to "our little party," or "my little business."

A good example of this subliminal language is in a news report giving the scores for a state high school basketball tournament. Girls' scores were given passively and negatively as:

> Central team lost to Midland School 87 to 77.
> Universal School was smothered by Senior School 97 to 65.

Conversely, the boys' scores were given actively and positively as:

> The Main Team won over the Majors 78 to 66.
> The Champs Team whipped the Scroungers 79 to 56.

Another example comes from a writers' group that was discussing inclusive language. Most of the group were women who debated the use of *author* and *authoress*. One writer commented, "What difference does it make? Why should I get bogged down with changing the language; I just get mixed up with he/ she; the whole thing is a bother."

Within minutes, another author remarked, "Every novel needs some bad guys in it. You even have to give *her* (referring to the antihero) some redeeming qualities." Are the villains assumed to be male; the *good guys* female?

And then, "The condition of *man* means us all." Really!

These examples of the assumed, subliminal, subconscious meanings of sexism in our language are the reasons that this entire subject is important. These are the reasons we need to be *bothered* by the meanings of our words, as authors, business people, and communicators in a society that must recognize the equality of women and men.

HABITS

Generalizing can be another habit that gets you into trouble with misleading assumptions like:

> Most women . . .
> Just like a woman!
> Old wives' tale
> A woman's place . . .
>
> *or*
> The defendant's lawyer was a woman, only 24.
>   (The implication is: "My, my, a woman!
>   capable! and young! imagine that!
>   incredible!")

Habits and habitual word usage are difficult to break and will require both care and attention. Have fun spotting an inaccurate or ludicrous remark that won't stand up under scrutiny for specific meaning. Don't make these remarks in your spoken English or let them appear in your papers, business literature, or correspondence, or in any writing that goes out with your name on it. Keep them from leaving your mouth by checking temptation with the question, "Would this apply to the other gender?" And as writers, check closely to be sure that you are using words to the best of your ability, exactly, specifically, to give your readers the meaning you wish to convey and not a meaning they must work to decipher.

One minister sent out a newsletter containing the statement, "Only man can sin." To which more than one woman in the congregation breathed a sigh of relief.

9 A Final Word

Language is constantly changing. In the past decade or two, some of the changes have involved discarding outworn language that refers inaccurately to differences between the sexes.

This is important, because language is a means to sharing understanding. And when terminology and the symbols of language cease to represent diminution of women and begin to reflect equality of traits and characteristics, language usage will more accurately be able to achieve that shared understanding.

Many excellent books have been and are being written by linguists on the subject of how sexism is reflected in language. Psychologists are writing about the effects of sexist language on both sexes. The purpose of *this* book is to offer some practical suggestions to remove sexist language from school papers, business literature, government writings, and other day-to-day usage. Using language that is not inclusive could produce illegal or costly results—*illegal* by ignoring affirmative-action programs, and *costly* by excluding half of your customers or potential customers: women.

Some of the problems will need time before they are solved uniformly across the land. Careful choice of words, awareness of cultural habits, and attention to the inequities will, in time, eliminate the misconceptions and inaccuracies that have been perpetuated through sloppy language usage and mindless cultural application.

Here are some final practical suggestions to ponder.

THINK OF WOMEN AS LEADERS

You may have heard the riddle about the lawyer's child who was rushed to the hospital, where the doctor couldn't operate because the child was identified as the doctor's own offspring. Learn to consider the possibility of women having prestigious, professional, and *nontraditional* roles. Women can be presidents, doctors, lawyers, chief executives, senators, pilots, line repairers, police officers, and insurance agents.

VISUALIZE ALL KINDS OF PEOPLE IN ALL KINDS OF ROLES

Secretaries, nurses, kindergarten teachers, and clerks all can be men. Managers, doctors, college professors, and bosses all can be women. It is time to rethink the assumption that power positions automatically belong to men and subordinate positions to women.

ORDER OF TERMS

Observe familiar terms and the order of listing and, once in awhile, reverse the order:

Change:	male and female	men and women
to:	female and male	women and men
Change:	boys and girls	husband and wife
to:	girls and boys	wife and husband

SUBSTITUTE NONSEXIST WORDS

Stay away from unnecessary masculine terms. Use male terms only when appropriate, not when referring to all humans, women and men. Replace such terms with accurate ones that better define your mental image, or remove the inappropriate terms altogether.

REMOVE THE MOUNTAIN!

Finally, if you can't go over the mountain, go around it, through it, or under it, or tear it down! If you can't repair a sexist phrase, cross it out and start over.

This is the bottom line: sexist (or inappropriate) language may be costing you friendship, harmony, money, sales, goodwill, or all of the above.

Glossary of Alternative Terms

actress actor
adman advertising agent, representative, ad person, creator, planner, layout person, adsmith, artist
administratrix *(Law)* administrator
adulteress adulterer
advanceman advance agent
adventuress adventurer
aircraftsman aviator, aircraft engineer, rocket engineer
airline stewardess airline steward, flight attendant
airman/woman pilot, aviator, flier
airmanship flying skill, aviation skill
alderman public official, council member
alumna, alumnae *(Latin)* *(do not use to include men)*
alumnus, alumni *(Latin)* *(do not use to include women)*
Amazon *(woman)* eliminate
ambassadress ambassador
anchorman anchor, reporter, editor
ape-man prehuman, missing link
assemblyman assemblyperson, assembly member; assembler, assembly worker
authoress author
aviatrix, aviatress aviator, flier, pilot

baby *(woman)* eliminate

baby doll *(woman)* eliminate
bachelor girl, bachelorette single woman, unmarried woman
bachelor's degree undergraduate degree
bag *(woman)* eliminate
bagboy bagger, grocer's assistant/helper
baggage man porter, checker
bailsman sponsor, bailer, bailperson
ball and chain *(woman)* eliminate
ballerina ballet dancer
bandsman instrumentalist, band player, band member
barman/maid bartender, barkeep, waiter
barmaster *(Brit.)* chancellor, squire, jurat, recorder
bastard *(man)* eliminate
bat *(woman)* eliminate
bathing beauty eliminate
batman *(Brit.)* orderly
battle-ax *(woman)* eliminate
beauty queen eliminate
beaver *(woman)* eliminate
bedfellow partner, associate, mate
bellboy bellhop, porter, messenger, helper
better half *(woman)* eliminate
big man personage, person of importance or greatness
birdman, man-bird aviator, pilot, flier
bitch *(woman)* eliminate

black widow *(woman)* eliminate

blindman blind person, unseeing person, visually impaired individual

blonde blond

blushing bride bride

boardman member of the board

boatman boater, rower, sailor, captain

bondsman guarantor, insurer, bondsperson

bookman scholar, author, librarian

bossman/lady boss, owner, partner, president

bowman archer, shooter

boyfriend *(man)* friend

boyish youthful

brakeman guard, railroad worker

brethren *(unrelated)* laity, congregation, assembly

brewmaster brew director, chief brewer, head brewer

bridesmaid bride's attendant

broad *(woman)* eliminate

brother *(unrelated)* friend, cohort, companion

brotherhood human kinship, camaraderie, community, esprit de corps

brotherly friendly, kind

brotherly love goodwill, charity, altruism, bigheartedness

brunette brunet

buck *(man)* eliminate

bull *(man)* eliminate

bull session meeting, get-together, talk-fest

bunny *(woman)* eliminate

busboy service worker, waiter's helper

Bushmen Bush people

businessman/woman executive, financier, entrepreneur, industrialist, tycoon, magnate, capitalist, leader, manager, owner, partner, businessperson *(also field of business, e.g.,* accountant, broker, marketer, agent, designer, architect, journalist, retailer, banker)

busman bus driver

busman's holiday vacation, long holiday

cabin boy crew member

cabman cab driver, cabby

call girl prostitute

cameraman, camera girl camera operator, photographer, video technician

career girl career person, careerist, diplomat, *or* career woman *to differentiate from* career man

cat *(woman)* eliminate

cattlemen cattle breeders, cattle owners, cattle herders

catty *(woman)* eliminate

cavemen cave dwellers, cave people *(appropriately defined, e.g.,* Neanderthal, Cro-Magnon, Australopithecus)

chairman *(verb)* chair, preside, administrate, officiate

chairman *(noun)* chair, chairperson, leader, speaker, convener, coordinator, facilitator, head, presiding officer, director

chambermaid housekeeper, servant, personal attendant

charwoman charworker, janitor

checkroom girl checkroom attendant

chessman chess piece (rook, castle, pawn, *etc.*)

chick (*woman*) *eliminate*

chickie-baby (*woman*) *eliminate*

Chinaman Chinese person

chippie (*woman*) *eliminate*

choirgirl/boy choir member, singer

chore boy/girl messenger, helper, attendant

chorus boy/girl member of the chorus, dancer, singer, performer

churchman churchwarden, elder, lay officer, acolyte

cigarette girl cigarette vendor

city fathers city council, leaders, officeholders, founders

clansman member of the clan

classman student, pupil, trainee

cleaning lady house cleaner, janitor, housekeeper

clergyman/woman pastor, minister, member of the clergy

clinging vine (*woman*) *eliminate*

clubwoman/man socialite, member

coachman driver

coastguardsman cadet, middy, coast guard

coed student

comedienne comedian, comic, humorist

committeeman committee member

common man commoner, average person

company man team player, loyal employee

concertmaster first violinist, concert leader

conductress conductor

confidante confidant

confidence man confidence-game player, cheat, swindler

Congressman/woman Member of Congress, Representative, Senator

contact man contact person, liaison

copy girl/boy copy carrier, messenger

copyman copy editor, copy writer, copy chief

coquette *eliminate*

costerman (*Brit.*) costermonger, vendor, peddler, hawker

councilman council member, councilor, representative

counterman/girl clerk, waiter

countryman compatriot, citizen, patriot

cow (*woman*) *eliminate*

cowboy/girl/man cowhand, cowkeeper, rider, cowpoke, cowpuncher

craftsman artist, artisan, skilled worker, accomplished crafts worker

craftsmanship skilled artistry, craft ability, experience, accomplishment, craftship (*like* authorship), handcraftship

crewman crew member

crone (*woman*) *eliminate*

dairyman dairy farmer, dairy worker, herder, dairy delivery driver

dame (*untitled woman*) *eliminate*

dancing girl dancer

danseuse danseur, dancer

dayman day worker, day laborer

deaconess deacon, elder

dear, dearie *use only in intimacy*

dear sir *(salutation) eliminate*

debutante debutant

deep-sea man saltwater sailor, deep-sea sailor, deep-sea diver

deliveryman delivery person, deliverer

directress director

dish *(woman) eliminate*

distaff *eliminate in reference to women*

divorcée divorcé

dog *(woman) eliminate*

doll *(woman) eliminate*

doorman door attendant, doorkeeper, porter, bell captain, valet

doughboy soldier

draftsman drafter, draftsperson, drawer

drayman wagoner, trucker

drum majorette baton twirler

dustman *(Brit.)* street sweeper

Dutchman Dutch person

elderman elder

elder statesman senior political leader, senior government leader

element's daughter *(Chem.)* offspring or descendent element *(elements of radioactive decay)*

emperor, empress ruler, monarch, sovereign, regent, commander, leader

enchantress enchanter, charmer, tempter

engineman engineer, engine driver

Englishman English person

enlisted man enlistee, recruit, member

equestrienne equestrian

errand boy messenger, courier

exciseman *(Brit.)* tax collector

executrix *(Law)* executor, administrator

expressman deliverer, transporter

exterminator man exterminator

fair sex *eliminate*

fallen woman *eliminate*

fall guy scapegoat, stand-in

family of man humankind, the human family

fancy man gigolo, pimp

fancy woman prostitute

farmerette farmer

fashion plate *(woman) eliminate*

father/master God Creator, Parent, Protector, Almighty Being, Power, Love, Holy One, God, Spirit

Father of Waters Mississippi River

fatherland homeland, native land

faultsman troubleshooter, maintenance person

favorite son favorite candidate

fellow friend, comrade, associate, peer, mate

fellowman kindred human being

fellowship foundation, provider, stipend, gift, fund

feminine rhyme *(Poetry, Music)* rhyme with an unstressed final syllable

ferryman ferryer

fiancée fiancé, betrothed, affianced

fickle *eliminate as a description of women*

fighting man soldier, fighter

filly *(girl) eliminate*

fireman fire fighter

first lady President's spouse; *refer to by name, e.g., Ms. or Mrs. Bush*

fisherman fisher, marine farmer, aquaculturist

fishwife *eliminate*

flag girl/man flagger, train guard, signaler

floorman floor walker, stockbroker

flower girl flower attendant

fluff *(girl)* *eliminate*

flyboy pilot, flier, aviator

footman valet, servant

forefather forebear, ancestor, foreparent, founder

forelady/man supervisor, overseer, chair, spokesperson, superintendent, jury foreperson, leader

forgotten man the unemployed, the poor, the underprivileged, the destitute

founding father founder, trailblazer, pioneer, innovator, forebear, ancestor

fox *(woman)* *eliminate*

fraternal twins nonidentical twins

fraternize socialize, associate with, consort with

freeman freeperson

Frenchman French person

freshman beginner, first-year student, novice, initiate

frogman diver, sailor, swimmer

frontiersman pioneer, leader, settler, forester, forerunner, explorer

front man mediator, intermediary

funnyman comedian, humorist, comic

G-man government employee, agent, police officer, detective

gagman writer, humorist

gal *use only for girls under 14*

gamesmanship game playing

garbageman recycler, garbage/trash collector, waste management engineer

gasman gas deliverer, attendant; anaesthesiologist

gateman gatekeeper, gate tender, security guard

geisha girl geisha, dancer

gentleman *use on par with* lady

gentlemen *do not use randomly as letter salutation*

gentlemen's agreement honorable agreement, handshake agreement, unwritten agreement, pact

girl *See Chapter 6; do not use to refer to things (animal, boat, car, etc.)*

girl (or gal) Friday secretary, assistant, receptionist

girlfriend *(woman)* friend

girlie *eliminate*

girlish youthful

glamor girl *eliminate*

goddess god

godfather/mother *use as appropriate*

God the Father See *father/master God*

goodwife wife, spouse

gossip *(woman)* *eliminate*

governess children's caretaker/nurse/sitter

gownsman gownsperson, professional or academic person

grandfather clause existing-condition clause

grandmother/father *use as appropriate*

granny *use only as endearing term for grandmother*

gray mare (*woman*) *eliminate*

great man great person, celebrity, personage, benefactor

groceryman grocer, clerk

guardsman guard, soldier

guildsman guild member, guildsperson, union member, cardholder

gunman shooter, killer, assassin, hoodlum, gunner

guy (*woman*) *eliminate*

hackman hackie, cab driver

hag (*woman*) *eliminate*

handicraftsman handicraftsperson

handmaid instrument, tool, agent, vehicle, medium

handyman handyperson, carpenter, plumber, electrician

hangman executioner

hardwareman retailer, hardware seller, sales clerk

harlot *eliminate*

harpy (*woman*) *eliminate*

hat-check girl hat-check attendant, hat checker

hatchetman hanger-on, killer, hoodlum, roughneck

he/she or **her/him** *See Chapter 4*

headman boss, owner, president, supervisor

headmaster principal

heifer (*woman*) *eliminate*

heiress heir

helmsman coxswain, guider, steerer

he-man man

hen (*woman*) *eliminate*

henchman right-hand helper, follower, adherent, flunky, hanger-on, right arm

hen party women's party

hen-pecked *eliminate*

herdboy, herdsman herder

heroine hero

highwayman robber, thief, vandal

history of man history

holdup man robber, thief, mugger

honey *use only in intimacy*

hooker (*woman*) prostitute

horseman horseback rider, trainer, horse breeder, equestrian

horsemanship ridership, equitation, skill

hostess host, attendant, social director

hotelman hotel operator, manager, desk clerk

housewife homemaker, householder

hoyden active child

hula girl hula dancer

hunk (*man*) *eliminate*

huntress hunter

huntsman hunter

hussy *eliminate*

ice-cream man ice-cream vendor, ice-cream seller

idea man idea person, creator, imaginative person

industrial man industrialist

infantryman infantry soldier, foot soldier

inner man inner self, inner person, psyche

inside man accomplice, undercover agent, spy, insider

insurance man insurance agent, representative

Irishman Irish person

jack-of-all-trades handy person, handy worker

jazz man musician, jazz player

Jewess Jew

Jezebel *(woman)* *eliminate*

jiggle *(woman)* *eliminate*

john *(man)* *eliminate*

john toilet, water closet, bathroom, restroom

johnny-on-the-spot prompt person

johnny-come-lately newcomer, new arrival, recruit

John Q. Public the public

journeyman experienced worker, journey-level (mid-level) tradeworker

junior miss *eliminate*

juryman juror, member of the jury

just like a woman *eliminate*

kept woman *eliminate*

kewpie doll *(woman)* *eliminate*

key man key person, key executive

kinglike regal, dignified, noble

kingmaker politically powerful person

kingpin political leader

king's English proper English

king-size large, huge

king's ransom valuable goods, huge sum

kinsmen kin, kinfolk, relatives

kitten *(woman)* *eliminate*

ladies' man *eliminate*

Lady Luck luck

Lady Nicotine tobacco

lady *(as in: lady judge, lady doctor, lady chef, etc.)* *eliminate (See Chapter 6)*

lady-killer *eliminate*

ladykin *eliminate*

ladylike define

lady of the evening *eliminate*

lady of the house *eliminate*

lady's auxiliary *eliminate*

lady's wind gentle breeze

landlord/lady owner, manager

laundress, laundryman laundry worker

lawman officer, sheriff, lawkeeper

layman lay person

layout man layout person

leading man/lady leading actor

leadman leader

learned man learned person, sage, scholar

leg man runner, messenger, reporter

letterman athlete of achievement, achiever

lighthouse man lighthouse keeper

lineman line installer, line repairer, line worker, electrical technician; train worker; football player

lioness lion

little lady *eliminate*

little woman wife

longshoreman stevedore, dock hand, loader

lookout man guard, sentry, lookout

loose woman *eliminate*

low man (on the totem pole) neophyte, beginner

lumberman, lumberjack logger, woodcutter, forester, ranger

madam *eliminate*

madman lunatic, maniac

maid houseworker, servant, attendant, domestic

maiden untried, first, early, single

maidenhood girlhood

maidenly *eliminate*

maiden name father's name, family name, birth name

maid of honor honored attendant, best woman

mailman postal carrier, mail carrier, letter carrier

maintenance man janitor, repair technician, upkeep technician

maître d' dining-room captain, head waiter

majorette major

make a new man of make a new person of

makeup man makeup person, makeup artist

male/female hardware couplings; plugs and sockets; *etc.*

mama's boy spoiled child

man *(noun)* See Chapter 3

man *(verb)* operate, tend, staff

man about town *eliminate*

manageress manager

man among men important person

man and wife wife and husband, *or* husband and wife

maneater cannibal, savage

man Friday servant, attendant, assistant

manful, manfulness *eliminate*

man from Mars creature from Mars

man from outer space creature from outer space

manhandle mishandle, maltreat

manhole utility hole, maintenance hatch, sewer, conduit

manhunt search, investigation

man hours work hours, time

man in the street average person, person in the street, common person

mankind humankind, humanity, people

manlike anthropomorphic, humanlike

manly, manliness *define*

manmade synthetic, artificial

mannish *explain*

man of action human dynamo, hustler, go-getter, enthusiast

man of God minister, pastor, holy person

man of goodwill peacemaker

man of letters academic, scholar

man of means person of means, rich person

man of straw nonentity, insignificant person

man of taste person of taste, sophisticate

man of the hour honored person

man of the world cosmopolitan person, citizen of the world

man of the year honored person, citizen of the year

man-of-war armed naval vessel, warship

man on horseback dictator, tyrant

man on the street common person, average person

man overboard someone's overboard, help!

manpower labor, work; crew, staff, personnel,

human-power, muscle-power

man's best friend dog

man-sized large

man's law the law

man's work work

man-to-man face-to-face, one-on-one, person-to-person

mare *(woman)* eliminate

marked man marked person, target

marksman shooter, sharpshooter, crack shot, dead-eye

marksmanship shooting proficiency

masculine rhyme *(Poetry, Music)* rhyme with a stressed or strong final syllable

masseuse masseur, massager, massage therapist

master expert, specialist; to achieve excellence

master/father *See* father

masterful skillful; imperious, arrogant

master key skeleton key, passkey

mastermind leader, intelligent planner, creator; to create

master of ceremony announcer, leader, coordinator

masterpiece great work of art

master plan blueprint, ground plan, working plan, plan of action, project design

master's degree graduate-level degree

master stroke bright idea, brilliant move

matron of honor honored attendant, best woman

mayoress mayor

meatman butcher, meat cutter

mechanical man robot, mechanical device, machine

medical man doctor, medical practitioner, physician

medicine man spirit healer, doctor, native doctor, shaman, faith healer

men *See Chapter 3*

men working people working, workers ahead, workers, work party

meter man/maid meter reader

metropolitan man sophisticate, urbanite

middleman negotiator, go-between, liaison, intermediary, contact person

midshipman cadet

milady *describe*

militiaman soldier, cadet

milkman milk deliverer, dairy worker, milk-truck driver

Miss Ms.

missy *eliminate*

mistress *eliminate (unless there is an equal term for men in the same position)*

modern man people today, modern humans

molly *(man)* *eliminate*

mother country native country, homeland

Mother Earth earth, world, globe

motherhood, fatherhood parenthood

motherland native country, homeland

motherlike *describe*

mother lode main lode

Mother Nature nature

mother's son parent's child

mother tongue native tongue

motorman driver; engineer
Mrs. Ms.
murderess murderer

nag *(woman)* *eliminate*
nanny children's caretaker/
nurse/sitter
needlewoman
needleworker, sewer
Negress Negro, Black
woman
new man new person
newsboy news deliverer,
news seller, news carrier
newsman reporter, anchor,
journalist
newspaperman editor,
reporter, journalist, copy
writer
night watchman night
guard, security guard, sentry
nobleman nobleperson,
member of the nobility
no man's land unowned or
uninhabited land, the wild
Norseman Norse person
nurseryman gardener,
horticulturist, florist,
landscape gardener, nursery
worker
nymphomaniac *eliminate*

oarsman rower
odd man extra person;
eccentric or unorthodox
person
office boy/girl office helper,
assistant, aide, runner
of the feminine persuasion
female
**of the masculine
persuasion** male
oilman oil executive, oil-field
worker
old lady *eliminate*
old maid single woman
old wives' tale superstition,
folklore

old-womanish *eliminate*
ombudsman researcher,
mediator
organization man loyal
employee, team player
outdoorsman outdoors
person, naturalist

paperboy paper carrier,
paper deliverer
patrolman patrol or police
officer, guard, sentry
patron, patroness sponsor,
backer, customer,
benefactor, donor, supporter
patronize protect, support,
benefit, back, donate, foster,
trade with; condescend to
paymaster cashier,
treasurer, accountant
Peeping Tom voyeur,
snoop, eavesdropper
penman writer; secretary,
copyist
penmanship handwriting,
script, hand, calligraphy
piece *(woman)* *eliminate*
pig *(woman)* *eliminate*
pinup girl *eliminate*
pit man theater prompter;
stockbroker
pitchman solicitor, barker,
salesperson
plainclothesman police
officer, detective, operative,
investigator, sleuth,
undercover officer
playboy/girl pleasure
seeker, reveler, merrymaker,
carouser
plowman/boy plower,
agriculturist, farmer, tiller
poetess poet
policeman police officer,
constable *(Brit.)*, detective
political man politician
poor man beggar, street
person

postman postal carrier, postal clerk, mail deliverer, postal employee

postmaster/mistress post office manager

powder puff *(woman) eliminate*

prehistoric man prehistoric people, humanlike primates, Stone (Ice, Bronze, Iron) Age people; the Neanderthals, the Cro-Magnons, *etc.*

pressman press operator, printer; newspaper person

priestess priest

prioress prior

prodigal son prodigal child *(except in biblical reference)*

proprietress proprietor

publicity man publicist

pussy *(woman) eliminate*

quail *(woman) eliminate*

queen bee *(woman) eliminate*

queenly dignified, regal, noble

queen's English proper English

radarman radar operator, radar technician, air-traffic controller

radioman radio operator, disk jockey

railroad man railroad worker, railroader, engineer

ranchman farmer, cattle raiser, rancher, ranch hand

rangeman range rider, ranger, range hand

reman restaff

Red Man Native American, American Indian

Renaissance man Renaissance person, individual with wide knowledge and skills

repairman repairer, technician

restaurant man restaurant owner, restaurateur

rewrite man rewriter, reviser

rib *(wife) eliminate*

rifleman shooter, soldier

right-hand man assistant, key person, right arm

rocket man rocketeer, astronaut

saleslady/man clerk, sales agent, representative

satyr *(man) eliminate*

satyriasis *eliminate*

scarlet woman *eliminate*

schoolboy/girl student, school child

schoolman academic, scholar, teacher, professor

schoolmarm *eliminate*

Scotchman Scotch person, Scot

scullery maid scullery worker

sculptress sculptor

seaman sailor, mariner

seamanship sailing ability, marine expertise

seamstress sewer, mender, garmentmaker

seductress seducer

seigneur person of rank, landowner

seigniorage rights of landowners

selectman representative, board officer

self-made man self-made person, entrepreneur

serviceman service member, member of the military, servicer, repairer, service/repair person; plumber, carpenter, electrician, *etc.*

sex kitten *eliminate*

sheepman sheep herder, sheep raiser, sheep rancher

she/he, her/him *See Chapter 4*

shepherdess shepherd

shipmaster commander, captain

shoeshine boy shoeshiner, bootblack

shopgirl shopkeeper, clerk

showman actor; director; producer

showmanship showiness, dramatism, stage presence

shrew *(woman) eliminate*

siren *(woman) eliminate*

sisterly *define*

sister plant nuclear power plant

sister ship co-ship

skipper's daughters *(Naut.)* whitecaps, rough sea

skirt *(woman) eliminate*

skirt chaser *eliminate*

sleeping beauty sleeper, sleepyhead

slut *eliminate*

snowman snow creation, snowperson

social man social person, mixer

softer sex *eliminate*

son-of-a-bitch *eliminate*

son-of-a-gun *eliminate*

son of the soil farmer, peasant

song-and-danceman singer and dancer

songstress singer

sons of God, sons of Martha, sons of the devil children of . . .

sorceress sorcerer

sound man sound technician

spaceman astronaut, cosmonaut

spinster *eliminate*

spinsterhood *eliminate*

spokesman spokesperson, speaker, representative

sportsman outdoorsperson, sportsperson; hunter, fisher, *etc.*

sportsmanship fair play

squaw *(woman) eliminate*

squeeze *(woman) eliminate*

stableboy/man stable tender, stable cleaner

stag *(man) eliminate*

stageman stagehand

stag party men's party

stallion *(man) eliminate*

starlet young star, young actor

statesman leader, diplomat, public figure, politician

statesmanship statecraft, diplomacy, leadership

stationmaster dispatcher, station operator, station official

steersman steerer, pilot, operator

stewardess steward, flight attendant

stockman stock raiser, stockkeeper

Stone Age Man Stone Age beings, primitives

straight man stooge, set-up

straw man weak adversary

streetwalker prostitute

striptease stripper

strongman giant, strongperson, bully, strongarm

stud *(man) eliminate*

stuntgirl/man stunt performer

suffragette suffragist

suffragettism suffrage

sugar *(woman) eliminate*

sugar daddy *eliminate*

suitor *(man) eliminate*

superioress superior

superman/woman superior being

sweetie *(woman)* *eliminate except as genderless intimate term*

switchman switcher, railroad worker

swordsman swordholder, combatant, fencer

tallyman, tallywoman tallier

T and A *(women)* *eliminate*

tart *(woman)* *eliminate*

taskmaster overseer, tyrant

taxman tax agent, tax preparer, tax consultant

telephone man telephone installer, telephone repairer, telephone service person

temptress tempter

testatrix *(Law)* testator

theaterman theater operator, theater manager, theater director, theater producer

the wife wife

tigress tiger

timberman timber worker, forester, woodcutter

to a man to a person

toastmaster/mistress head speaker, toastmaker, coordinator, announcer

tomato *(woman)* *eliminate*

tomboy active child

tomcat *(man)* *eliminate*

Tom, Dick, and Harry everyone, ordinary people, people in general

tootsie *eliminate*

townsman townsperson, citizen

tradeswoman/man tradesperson, trader, vendor

trainman, trainmaster conductor, switcher, dispatcher, engineer

tramp *(woman)* *eliminate*

traveling man traveling person, salesperson

trencherman hearty eater

tribesman member of a tribe

trigger man assassin, hoodlum

trollop *eliminate*

turfman jockey, rider, horse racer

two-man, three-man, *etc.* two-seated, two-person, *etc.*

Uncle Sam U.S. *or* United States government

Uncle Tom *eliminate*

underclassman undergraduate, member of the lower levels

undercoverman undercover agent, officer

unfeminine *eliminate*

union man union member, union worker, card holder

unladylike *eliminate*

unmanly *eliminate*

unwed mother mother

upperclassman member of the junior or senior (upper) class, older student

usherette usher

utility man general utility, utility person

vamp *(woman)* *eliminate*

vestal virgin *eliminate*

vice chairman vice chair

victress victor

villainess villain

virgin *(woman)* *eliminate*

virginal, virginhood *eliminate in reference to women*

vixen *(woman)* *eliminate*

waitress waiter, wait person, service person

wallflower *(woman)* *eliminate*

war horse *(woman)* *eliminate*

war paint (*cosmetics*)
 eliminate
washerwoman washer,
 launderer
watchman guard,
 watchkeeper
water boy water carrier
waterman boater, rower
weak sister weakling,
 coward
weaker sex *eliminate*
wear the pants dominate,
 take the lead
weatherman/girl
 weathercaster, forecaster,
 meteorologist, weather
 reporter
well done, for a woman
 well done
Welshman Welsh person
wench (*woman*) *eliminate*
wenching *eliminate*
wheelsman steerer, pilot
whipping boy scapegoat
white man Caucasian, white
 person
whore prostitute
widower, widowman
 widow
wifely *explain; should not be
 used to mean* obedient,
 faithful, compliant
wild man wild person
wingman pilot, flier, aviator
wise guy wisecracker,
 jokester
wise man sage, wise person,
 learned one
witch (*woman*) *eliminate*
wolf (*man*) *eliminate*
**woman architect, painter,
 driver, boater, etc.**
 architect, painter, driver,
 boater, *etc.*

woman chaser, womanizer
 eliminate
woman of the street
 prostitute
woman's auxiliary
 eliminate
woman's place *eliminate or
 designate*
woman's work work
womanish, womanly
 define, explain
woodsman forester, timber
 worker, outdoorsperson,
 hunter
working mother worker,
 employed person, laborer
working man worker,
 laborer, employed person
workman worker, laborer,
 attendant; *describe field of
 work* (as deliverer, line
 worker, production worker,
 etc.)
workmanlike skillful
workmanship expertise,
 skill
workmen's compensation
 workers' compensation

yachtsman yachter, boater,
 captain, skipper
yardman yard worker,
 landscaper
yardmaster yard operator,
 manager
yeoman attendant, assistant,
 clerk, farmer, guard
yes man endorser,
 supporter, follower
yokefellow companion, co-
 worker
young man youth, teenager

Index